THE

ROSARY

HANDBOOK

A GUIDE FOR NEWCOMERS, OLD-TIMERS, AND THOSE IN BETWEEN

REVISED AND UPDATED

THE
ROSARY
HANDBOOK

A GUIDE FOR
NEWCOMERS, OLD-TIMERS,
AND THOSE IN BETWEEN

REVISED AND UPDATED

MITCH FINLEY

the**WORD**
among us®
press

Published by The Word Among Us Press
7115 Guilford Road
Frederick, Maryland 21704
www.wau.org

21 20 19 18 17   1 2 3 4 5

ISBN: 978-1-59325-321-9
eISBN: 978-1-59325-501-5

Unless otherwise noted, Scripture passages contained herein are from
the New Revised Standard Version Bible: Catholic Edition, copyright ©
1989, 1993 Division of Christian Education of the National Council of
the Churches of Christ in the United States. All rights reserved.
Used with permission.

Quotations are taken from the English translation of the *Catechism of
the Catholic Church* for the United States of America (indicated as CCC),
Second Edition, copyright © 1997 by the United States Catholic Confer-
ence—Libreria Editrice Vaticana.

Unless otherwise noted, quotations from Vatican documents
are from the Vatican website, Vatican.va.

Cover design by Faceout Studios

Made and printed in the United States of America
Library of Congress Control Number: 2017944418

CONTENTS

I dedicate this new edition to my wife and dearest friend, Kathy Finley.

THE ROSARY AND YOU:
A PERFECT MATCH

My earliest memories of the Rosary are from the school year of 1953–54, when I was in the third grade. This was the first year that I attended a Catholic school, which happened to be Saints Peter and Paul School in the small north-central Idaho town of Grangeville. Benedictine Sisters from the Monastery of St. Gertrude, from nearby Cottonwood, Idaho, served as our teachers.

Our parents enrolled my younger sister and me in this little Catholic school even though we weren't Catholic. Less than two years later, however, the four of us stood over the baptismal font in the back of Saints Peter and Paul Church, as the pastor, Fr. Thomas Lafey, poured the waters of baptism over our heads. For me, it was the beginning of a lifelong love affair with Catholicism and—I was soon to discover—with the Rosary as well.

Some years ago, I returned to Saints Peter and Paul School, and I could still pinpoint the place in the school's gymnasium where I stood one May morning—May being the month of the Blessed Virgin Mary—as a non-Catholic third grader, when one of the sisters designated me, along with some sixty other fidgeting kids, to represent one of the beads of a rosary. We were going to become, Sister said, a "living rosary."

(Throughout this book, I capitalize "Rosary" whenever I refer to the prayer form that is called "*the* Rosary." When I refer to a circlet of beads or other counter called "*a* rosary," I spell "rosary" with a lowercase "r.")

The idea was that each student would begin the prayer to be said for the bead that he or she represented, and then everyone would join in to complete the prayer until we had prayed all five decades of a complete Rosary. I was designated as a "Hail Mary," but not being Catholic then, I had little clue as to how to recite one. As I recall, I represented one of the beads toward the end of the second or third decade. I listened closely as the kids before me prayed aloud, "Hail Mary, full of grace, the Lord is with thee; blessed art thou among women, and blessed is the fruit of thy womb, Jesus." The entire assembly would then complete the prayer: "Holy Mary, Mother of God, pray for us sinners now and at the hour of our death. Amen."

I hadn't a clue what "fruit of thy womb" might mean, but it didn't seem to bother anyone else, so why should I let it bother me? When my turn came, I recited the opening words of the prayer correctly—more or less. To my relief, the Rosary continued with no major breakdown. The Rosary became part of my life from then on—it was a taken-for-granted part of being Catholic.

Years later, after graduating from a Catholic high school in 1964, I joined the US Navy, and one of the everyday ways I stayed in touch with my religious roots was through the Rosary. During the last of my four years in the Navy, in January 1968, I took a week's leave and flew from Norfolk, Virginia, where I was stationed at the naval air station, to Louisville, Kentucky. From there, by bus, I traveled to Bardstown, Kentucky, and then got a ride out to the famous Trappist Abbey of Gethsemani, where I attended a weekend retreat. The white snows of winter lay all around, and the first day I was there, I bought a good, sturdy rosary in the monastery's gift shop—one I have to this day.

During my years in the Navy, I formed the habit of taking long walks most evenings, around whatever naval air station I was attached to at the time. I walked with a rosary in my jacket pocket, and I prayed as my fingers moved slowly from one bead to the next. And so I managed to keep some semblance of a spirituality alive and kicking. Indeed, without being conscious of it, I became an amateur contemplative, for the Rosary is a prayer that lends itself to meditation on many levels—some of which we may be hardly aware of. But I'm getting ahead of myself . . .

What's your story about the Rosary in your life? If you're a lifelong Catholic, you may have grown up in a family that prayed the Rosary together regularly at home or maybe during Advent or Lent. Perhaps you have been praying the Rosary faithfully for many years. Then again, you might be considering returning to the Rosary after not having prayed it for a long time. Or maybe you never really learned to pray the Rosary before, and now you're wondering whether it's for you.

Maybe you grew up in the years right after the Catholic Church's Second Vatican Council, in the mid-1960s, when the Rosary fell into disuse among many Catholics, and now you want to try it. If you've recently become Catholic—or even if you're just thinking about it—you may want to find out what the Rosary is all about. Whatever place the Rosary has in your life, and whatever your reason for picking up this book, this is the book that will help you learn about, rediscover, or enrich your experience with the Rosary.

Why Another Book on the Rosary

If you look around for books on the Rosary, soon you'll discover that there are more than a few available. Some are primarily devotional in nature. Others are semi-scholarly or popular studies of the Rosary. Some offer adaptations of the Rosary that incorporate Scripture into the prayer more than the conventional practice does. Others adapt the Rosary to a recovery-based spirituality.

There really isn't any "wrong" way to pray the Rosary—but if you're looking for frills, you won't find them here. Apart from a look, in the appendix, at some alternative ways to pray the Rosary or to pray other prayers using the beads of the rosary or similar beads, this book will focus on the standard, straightforward, "no-frills" prayer that has been used for generation after generation.

The Rosary Handbook isn't just another book on the Rosary. My first aim in writing it was to provide a fresh perspective on the Rosary by looking at this age-old devotional prayer through a thoroughly contemporary lens. I didn't want to merely repeat an understanding of the Rosary taken for granted by earlier generations. A great deal has happened in the Catholic Church since the mid-1960s. Significant theological discussions developed and continue to this day. In particular, Vatican II sparked a renewed Catholic understanding of the role of Mary in the Church and in salvation history, and this developing understanding sheds new light on the Rosary and other Marian devotions.

This book will discuss the Rosary in the light of twenty-first-century Catholic perspectives on Mary.

I wanted, also, to write a book about the Rosary that would convey and encourage the joy of praying this beloved prayer. Here, a grim or inappropriately solemn understanding of the Rosary won't be allowed to get even its toe in the door. The Blessed Mother is a joyful part of Catholic spirituality and devotional life, and the Rosary is a joyful prayer. It is true that one can be a good Catholic and have little or no devotion to the mother of Jesus. Still, it's the rare Catholic who has no warm feelings whatsoever for the Blessed Virgin Mary.

In addition, I want to show that the Rosary is a prayer for everyone—old and young, clergy and laity, those who pray daily and those who have trouble finding the time. Note too that this book disregards the sentimental devotionalism with which Mary and the Rosary have sometimes been viewed—and with which I, for one, am not comfortable. The Rosary and the Mary of this book will never be sticky sweet.

Finally, I want to provide a practical guide for prayer, not a recipe for a desired outcome. Some resources and styles of piety convey a kind of magical view of the Rosary. For example, there are narratives of the "true story" genre that imply that you can guarantee a loved one's safety by praying the Rosary for him or her every day. You may have read stories about parents who prayed the Rosary daily while an offspring in the military served in one combat zone or another—and he or she returned home unharmed. I dare say, however, that there are also parents who prayed the Rosary each day whose son or daughter did not come home safe and sound.

God answers our prayers in his own way and in his own time, which may or may not conform to our desires—whether we pray the Rosary or any other prayer. There are certainly benefits for us in praying the Rosary, but only God can determine the answers to our prayers.

Who Should Pray the Rosary?

Although there are many different reasons people have a fondness for particular prayers, I believe that there are several reasons why nearly everyone will find something they like in the Rosary. First, the Rosary this book encourages and celebrates is a devotional prayer suited to many situations and circumstances. When I say that the Rosary is devotional, I mean that it is what all prayer is: an intentional turning to the Divine Presence, to the loving God, Creator, Source, and Goal of all life, who—to paraphrase St. Augustine (AD 354–430)—is closer to us than we are to ourselves. Like all methods of prayer, the Rosary is a way to be with the God whom Scripture tells us "is love" (1 John 4:16).

The Rosary is a simple, uncomplicated, nonliturgical way to pray when conscious thoughts and words may fail you, no matter what your feelings or emotions may be at the moment. If you are depressed, the Rosary works. If you are happy or sad, the Rosary works. If you are bored, the Rosary works. If you are anxious or worried, the Rosary works. If you are sick or just plain sick and tired, the Rosary works. No matter how you're feeling, the Rosary is a way to be physically and intentionally in the presence of the triune God—Father, Son, and Holy Spirit—in the company of the Blessed Virgin Mary, the mother of the risen Christ and, through the Sacrament of Baptism in Christ, our mother too.

Another reason that the Rosary has something to offer just about everyone is that the Rosary is at once simple and deep. It is so simple that the humblest believers love the Rosary. It is so deep that many of the greatest thinkers and mystics down through the centuries have loved the Rosary. Indeed, the simplicity and depth of the Rosary are the simplicity and depth of the gospel itself, the good news of God's love and forgiveness for all in Christ. The combination of traditional prayers and meditation on sacred events makes the Rosary a particularly personal prayer that can be as uncomplicated or as complicated as you want to make it. Thus, it suits just about anyone's spirituality. In other words, chances are that the Rosary is a perfect match for you, no matter the characteristics of your personal spirituality.

At the same time, we must admit that the Rosary doesn't suit everyone. Even the occasional saint declared that he or she just couldn't pray the Rosary. Such saints and ordinary believers tend to be the exception, however, so give the Rosary a fair try before you decide one way or the other.

I hope that by this point I have your attention, and I hope that I have aroused your curiosity. A wonderful pilgrimage of discovery is ahead of us, one that I pray will lead us all closer to the risen Lord and to his—and our—Blessed Mother. Let us begin with joy and with hope.

CHAPTER 1

WHAT'S IN IT FOR ME?

Why You Should Pray the Rosary

I remember well the years right after the Second Vatican Council. The second half of the 1960s was an interesting time to be a Catholic—to say the least. One never knew what to expect next. Practically overnight the Mass became, in its appearance at least, remarkably different from what it had been for as long as anyone alive—not to mention the grandparents and great-grandparents of anyone alive—could remember.

The baccalaureate Mass for my 1964 Catholic high school graduation was the standard pre–Vatican II Mass, in which priest and assembly faced in the same direction, and all the prayers were in Latin. Within a few short years, however, priest and assembly faced each other, and the priest and the people in the pews spoke the prayers of the Mass in language everyone understood. Most important, the emphasis of the activity of the Mass shifted. The people in the pews were no longer mere observers of what the presider did at the altar but were now active participants in the liturgy.

During the decades prior to Vatican II, it was not uncommon for people to pray the Rosary during Mass. Everyone was encouraged to follow the prayers of the Mass in a personal missal, and many did so. But it wasn't unusual to see someone with beads in hand, silently praying the Rosary as the priest said Mass in Latin and as the altar boys (never girls!) responded in Latin, which most understood poorly, on behalf of the congregation. Once the "aftershocks" of Vatican II hit, however, Catholics got the message—either directly or indirectly—that praying the Rosary during Mass was definitely not okay. Further, for a good many years after Vatican II, the idea of praying the Rosary any time at all fell into disfavor among many Catholics.

Thinking back, I doubt that I held a rosary in my hands from about 1970 until 1985. That excellent old rosary I bought at the Abbey of Gethsemani lay neglected in the back of a drawer for all those years. Then, for mysterious reasons of the heart and the movement of divine grace, I returned to the Rosary.

The Rosary Is a Balanced Prayer

During the fifteen years that I wasn't praying the Rosary, I was active in my faith. Not only did I participate in the Mass regularly, but I earned degrees in theology and wrote many books and articles on popular theological topics. Time passed, however, and I began to sense that my faith, although intellectually vibrant, lacked an affective, devotional component. Believing it was time for me to reintegrate my feelings into my spirituality and include a devotional component in my prayer, I returned to the Rosary.

As it turned out, I couldn't have been happier with the results. A faith with an active affective component is a balanced, healthy faith. Without it, faith may become little more than a "head trip" or little more than a habit of going through the motions.

The last thing I would want to do is denigrate the place of the intellect in faith. There are far too many great saints who were intellectuals to do that. Authentic faith should never lead us to stop thinking or to neglect the critical intellectual faculties God has given us.

At the same time, mature faith includes an affective, or feeling, dimension. Our emotions belong in our faith and spirituality too. That's why devotional practices belong in the everyday life of faith—and one of the best and most time-honored of these, for Catholics especially, is the Rosary.

The Rosary Is a Comprehensive Prayer

Not only is the Rosary an excellent way to give faith a healthy affective component, it is also a theologically comprehensive prayer. Apart from the Mass, the Rosary is the most fully Christian devotional prayer available to us. In a very real sense, it has everything that is most basic to a Christian outlook on life and the world: a prayerful gesture invoking and placing ourselves in the presence of the triune God (Sign of the Cross); the most ancient creed, or statement of Christian faith, that we have (Apostles' Creed); the prayer that Jesus himself gives us in the Gospels of Matthew and Luke (Our Father); reminders of the key events in the life, death, and resurrection of Jesus and of his and our Blessed Mother (mysteries); petitionary prayers to Mary (Hail Mary); prayers of praise to the God who is Father, Son, and Holy Spirit (Glory Be); and a concluding prayer invoking, praising, and petitioning the prayers of the Blessed Virgin Mary. The Hail Holy Queen, also called the Salve Regina, and the Memorare, "Remember, O Most Gracious Virgin Mary . . . ," may be the most popular.

The Rosary is also particularly Catholic—and not just because it's mostly Catholics who pray it. The occasional Protestant Christian prays the Rosary, it's true, but this is a rare occurrence. If anything is likely to identify you to others as a Catholic, it will be to have a rosary in your possession.

The Rosary is especially Catholic because it draws upon what Catholics consider the two inseparable sources of divine revelation, Scripture and sacred Tradition—another sign of the Rosary's theological balance. All but two of the twenty mysteries, or sacred events, on which the prayers of the Rosary focus come directly from the Gospels, and the other two (the fourth and fifth glorious mysteries) come from sacred Tradition.

In order to better understand the interdependence of Scripture and Tradition, we first need to grasp the nature and importance of the latter. "Sacred Tradition" is the term we use to refer to the living transmission of all the beliefs, doctrines, rituals, Scriptures, and life of the Church. Quoting the Second Vatican Council's document on divine revelation, the *Catechism of the Catholic Church* declares that "through Tradition, 'the Church, in her doctrine, life, and worship, perpetuates and transmits to every generation all that she herself is, all that she believes'" (CCC 78).

We usually distinguish between sacred Tradition (capital "T") and individual traditions (lowercase "t"), which are the various customary practices "adapted to different places and times, in which the great Tradition is expressed" (CCC 83). One example of a lowercase "t" tradition is, of course, the Rosary.

Sacred Tradition is the life of the Church—meaning all of us—from the beginning down to the present day. It is the Christian community's ongoing experience and understanding of the risen Christ throughout the centuries. More, it is all the true and authentic consequences of that experience.

As our definition above notes, one of the first and most basic expressions of Tradition is Scripture itself. For it was the early Church's experience of and reflection on the Church's foundational events—in particular, the conception, birth, life, teachings, death, and resurrection of Jesus—that resulted in or gave birth to the New Testament. Indeed, it is part of sacred Tradition that the Bible as we know it includes the documents that it does and no others. Hence, all who accept the Christian Bible, whether they realize it or not, accept sacred Tradition too.

Pope Benedict XVI explained in his general audience of April 26, 2006,

> Tradition is the communion of the faithful gathered around the legitimate shepherds [i.e., the bishops] throughout history, a communion which the Holy Spirit nourishes, guaranteeing a connection between the experience of apostolic faith lived by the original community of disciples and the present experience of Christ in his Church.[1]

Beautifully illustrating that connection, the pope went on to say that "Tradition is a living river" connecting the faithful to Christ.

In other words, sacred Tradition did not cease once the canon of Scripture had been established, roughly speaking, in the late fourth century. The "communion of the faithful" with the risen Lord, "gathered around the legitimate shepherds," continued and continues today, and the development of the Church's understanding of that experience has gone hand in hand with it. Rooted in Scripture and Tradition, the Rosary is a living prayer that nourishes our intimacy with the living, risen Christ, who is continually revealed to us through Scripture, the Eucharist, and the other sacraments.

The Rosary Is a Christ-Centered Prayer in the Context of the Communion of Saints

Part of the Church's ongoing reflection on its faith experience relates to the place of Mary, the mother of Jesus, in the life of the Church. Non-Catholic Christians sometimes use the Rosary as evidence that Catholics give to a mere human being the adoration appropriate to God alone. Of course, Catholics know better. Authentic Catholicism *venerates* Mary; we do not worship or adore her. God alone is worthy of worship and adoration.

Moreover, the Rosary—although it has a Marian character—is a Christ-centered prayer. The Rosary focuses on what theologians call "the Christ event," that is, the life, ministry, death, and resurrection of Jesus. It is a devotional prayer designed to bring these events to our attention, time and again, because they are key moments in the history of salvation and, for Christians, the foundational events in the history of the Christian community. What better form of prayer for anyone who calls himself or herself a disciple of the risen Lord?

As the mother of our Lord and, in fact, his first disciple, Mary played an important part in the development of the Church, and veneration of her is part of the sacred Tradition of the Church as handed down to us from the apostles.

Essentially, the veneration of Mary belongs in the context of the Catholic doctrine of the communion of saints. In a nutshell, this doctrine says that the community of faith that is the Church transcends space and time. Therefore, we belong to a community that exists in both this world and the next, a community made up of all those who strive, by God's grace (God's self-gift), to live as disciples of Christ in this world plus the countless imperfect but faithful disciples of Christ who have gone before us into eternity. Some hold a special place of honor in the public life of the Church, beginning with the Blessed Virgin Mary, the mother of Jesus.

Just as we ask for one another's prayers in this world, so we can and should petition the saints in heaven to pray for us as well—and logically enough, the first among the saints, the Blessed Virgin Mary, holds a special place among those whose prayers we request. Our prayer for our mother Mary's intercession is, in its nature, no different from our requests for one another's prayers. The only unique characteristic of prayer to Mary, or to any of the saints, is whom we ask to pray for us. Just as we place a special value on the prayers of an especially holy person in this life, so we place an even greater value on the prayers of the saints—and first among them is the mother of the risen Lord.

When we pray the Rosary, we explicitly locate ourselves in the midst of this vast eternal community, and we petition our

Blessed Mother for her prayers on our behalf and on behalf of all those we pray for. In this sense, to pray the Rosary is to pray with and in the whole Church—the Church in this world and in eternity, the earthly Church and the heavenly Church. Theologically, one of the activities we engage in when we pray the Rosary is to celebrate the reality to which the Church's doctrine of the communion of saints refers.

The context of the Rosary, therefore, is the community of the Church existing in time and space and eternity. But the focus and center of the Rosary is Christ Jesus, the Lord of time and space and the Lord of eternity. It is to him that the Rosary directs us, and it is in his presence that the Rosary places us—in the company of his, and our, Blessed Mother.

The Rosary Is a Spiritually Nourishing Prayer

The fact that the Rosary directs our prayer to Christ in the company of his mother is healthy for the spirituality of men and the spirituality of women—for different but complementary reasons. The Rosary nourishes in the spiritualities of both men and women a healthy feminine dimension, because it is a Christ-centered prayer in a Marian, and therefore feminine, context. That is, the focus of the Rosary is on Christ, but the primary building block of the Rosary—the Hail Mary—praises the Blessed Virgin and petitions her for prayers on our behalf.

For men, praying the Rosary cultivates a deeper appreciation and respect for all things feminine. Through each Hail Mary, the Rosary places a man in the spiritual and real presence of the woman who became, and remains, the mother of Christ—in the original Greek of the fourth-century Nicene Creed, the

Theotokos, or Mother of God. A particular young woman was critically important in the working out of our salvation precisely because she was and remains a woman.

Thus, all women—because they are women—share in the honor and dignity of that one young woman. It was a young woman—by today's standards a mere girl—that the Creator of the universe chose and upon whose word he waited before the course of salvation could continue.

For a man to pray the Rosary is to open himself to the woman Mary. And because all women share in the dignity of Mary's womanhood, the man who prays the Rosary—if he truly understands what he is doing and remains open to the truth of what he is doing—cannot help but grow in sensitivity to the dignity of all women, in particular the women with whom he lives and works.

Such a man gradually deepens his ability to love and respect his wife, if he is married; his sisters, if he has any; and the women with whom he works—indeed, all women who cross his path each day. They express the same feminine qualities as the mother of the Son of God himself. And so, for a man who prays the Rosary and understands what he is doing, it would be impossible to disrespect or denigrate women in any way or to think of them as in any way inferior to himself.

If the Rosary leads the male heart to honor, welcome, and respect women as equal and complementary beings, the Rosary leads women—for the same reasons—to respect and honor themselves precisely because they are women. For a woman, to pray the Rosary is to place herself in the spiritual and real presence of the woman whose profoundly simple—yet far from simple-minded—faith made possible God's plan for the salvation of the world. The God of Israel beckoned her but left her free to choose as she would. Her yes to God is a model for all of us—women and men—to say yes to whatever God's plan is for our lives. When a woman consciously places herself in the presence of this strong, gentle, no-nonsense, wise, delightfully surprising woman, she opens herself to the influence and guidance of this woman who so bravely cooperated with the will and plan of God.

A woman who prays the Rosary is a woman who sees no reason to think of herself as inferior to anyone, regardless of gender. She treasures the gift of her feminine nature as equal in dignity and complementary to the masculine nature of men. The last thing a woman who prays the Rosary is likely to do—if she understands fully what she is doing—is to become a doormat for any man, no matter what assumptions some men carry around in their heads about women.

In an era when violence against women—physical and otherwise—is not uncommon, the Rosary can and should be for women a source of strength and of the power to embrace and nourish their God-given dignity. Women can pray the Rosary knowing that the woman interceding for them understands what it means to be a woman.

In other words—astonishing as it may be to some—the Rosary is a feminist prayer, and women and men who pray and live it are feminists in the best and truest sense of the word.

Feminism means taking for granted that woman and man are meant to complement each other while sharing equal dignity, equal freedom, and equal humanity—nothing more and nothing less. And feminists are men and women who are ready to stand up and work in practical, adult, no-nonsense ways to bring about acknowledgment of this equality in places and situations where it is ignored, denied, or overlooked, no matter by whom. Of course, "feminist" does not refer here to anyone who thinks of women as superior to men, any more than one should think of men as superior to women.

To say that the Rosary is a feminist prayer means that those who pray the Rosary acknowledge the equality and complementarity of women and men and are prepared to live out and work with that equality and complementarity. It does not mean, however, that those who pray the Rosary know the solutions or answers to the practical theological questions and issues that relate to gender roles in a given society and culture or even in the Church.

Indeed, those who pray the Rosary are perhaps more likely than others to be willing to eschew dogmatism, whether from the left or from the right, because to pray the Rosary is to open oneself to the ultimate mystery of the Incarnation—the entering into human nature and human history of the divine mystery that we call God and that the First Letter of John (4:8) identifies as love itself. To open oneself to this mystery is to know a love that fills the deepest recesses of the human heart, because it far transcends the human intellect. Therefore, dogmatism—in effect, an implicit, arrogant claim to personal infallibility—is no longer an option. Only humble adoration and a silent tongue constitute an appropriate response to this love and this mystery.

Praying the Rosary is spiritually and psychologically healthy for both men and women. It is so for men because the Rosary steeps a man's heart and soul in the feminine dignity and presence of the woman Mary. It is so for women because the Rosary steeps a woman's heart and soul in the feminine dignity and presence of the woman Mary. Men who pray the Rosary with understanding grow to respect and honor all women more. Women who pray the Rosary with understanding grow to respect and honor themselves more.

The Rosary Is a Human, Earthy Prayer

But there is still more to be said about the value of praying the Rosary. Another important reason to pray the Rosary is its incarnational nature. Because by custom the Rosary almost always includes the use of rosary beads, or some substitute for rosary beads, the Rosary is a wonderfully tactile way to pray.

To pray with a rosary is to have something to grab on to. Thus, prayer becomes more than a matter of thought, words, and bodily posture; it becomes a physical activity. You hold the circlet of beads, you feel the beads with your fingers, and you move the beads through your hands, from one to the next. Your hands pray as much as your mind, your words, and the rest of your body. So the Rosary is an embodied form of prayer because it involves your sense of touch.

At times of particular sadness or anxiety, or moments of special happiness or rejoicing, it can be comforting to have the prayer beads of a rosary to cling to, to hang on to, to help you focus. That's one reason, no doubt, that the Rosary remains so popular after so many centuries, with so many people of faith.

It's also true that the Rosary falls into the rhythmic, repetitive kind of prayer that Eastern religions refer to as "mantric." That is, it utilizes the repetition of a single prayer in order to help the person praying to both focus his or her attention and go deeper. The "over and overness" of the Hail Mary, especially, gives the mind—and when prayed aloud, the tongue—something to do.

The human mind tends to be like a popcorn popper: pop-pop-pop-pop, thoughts, ideas, and nonsense going off randomly in all directions, often uncontrollably, when the intention is to pray. While the conscious mind is occupying itself with the repetition of the Hail Mary, the heart, one's deeper center, can slip into the presence of our source and ultimate goal: the tri-une God, Father, Son, and Holy Spirit, who is love, compassion, mercy, forgiveness, and healing peace.

But, you might ask, in using repetitive prayer, are we guilty of violating the words of Jesus in the Gospel of Matthew: "When you are praying, do not heap up empty phrases as the Gentiles do; for they think that they will be heard because of their many words" (6:7)? Fortunately, because of the teachings of the Church as well as the insights of Scripture scholarship, we know that the answer to that question is no. The point of Jesus' words in the Gospel is to remind us that we don't need to repeat our requests to God over and over again out of a concern that God might not hear us.

That is not the purpose of the repetitive prayers of the Rosary. The repetition is for our sake, not God's. We repeat the Hail Mary simply as a way to maintain some focus during our prayer and to nourish what we might call a "state of prayerfulness." It has nothing to do with thinking that if we repeat the prayers of the Rosary, God will hear us because of our "many words."

Repetition, of itself, is perfectly understandable and good. When an audience applauds performers, their applause would seem ridiculous if it consisted of one single clap. No, applause consists of many claps, over and over. We might even say that the repetitive praying of the Hail Mary in the Rosary is one way we applaud Mary for her courageous, trusting faith. One Hail Mary just wouldn't do it!

Finally, some may remind us that we should pray the Rosary because the Blessed Virgin Mary herself, in various apparitions, instructed us to do so. This is a reason not without value and importance, to be sure. At the same time, we must remember that the Catholic Church does not require that we accept or believe in apparitions validated by Church authorities. For those who accept with gratitude and joy the authenticity of the Marian apparitions at, for example, Fátima and Lourdes, the Blessed Mother's admonitions to pray the Rosary are welcome. But we must keep in mind that, even based on these apparitions, we never have a right to get pushy about the Rosary with anyone, not even other Catholics. More about this later in the book.

Pray the Rosary for any or all of the reasons discussed in this chapter. To put it simply, we can say that praying the Rosary is a good idea because it is such a balanced, comprehensive, Christ-centered, spiritually nourishing, thoroughly human way to pray.

Mental Benefits of the Rosary

- increased focus and attention
- mental clarity, freedom from distractions and negative thoughts
- better thought control and fewer intrusive thoughts
- victory over depression
- improved memory (short-term and long-term)
- decreased anxiety and fear
- positive thinking and better outlook on life
- stress reduction
- increased ability to relax and unwind
- better and more restful sleep
- overall sense of well-being[2]

Inspiring Words on the Rosary

I would never do without the Rosary.

—Fr. Thomas Merton, OCSO

You will be surprised how you can climb out of your worries, bead by bead, up to the very throne of the Heart of Love itself.

—Archbishop Fulton Sheen

The greatest method of praying is to pray the Rosary.

—St. Francis de Sales

You always leave the Rosary for later, and you end up not saying it at all because you are sleepy. If there is no other time, say it in the street without letting anybody notice it. It will, moreover, help you to have [the] presence of God.

—St. Josemaría Escrivá

The Rosary is the most excellent form of prayer and the most efficacious means of attaining eternal life. It is the remedy for all our evils, the root of all our blessings. There is no more excellent way of praying.

—Pope Leo XIII

Never will anyone who says his Rosary every day be led astray. This is a statement that I would gladly sign with my blood.

—St. Louis de Montfort

In all the free time you have, once you have finished your duties of state, you should kneel down and pray the Rosary. Pray the Rosary before the Blessed Sacrament or before a crucifix.

—St. (Padre) Pio of Pietrelcina

Hear me out, the Rosary . . . Do you pray the Rosary each day? I don't know, are you sure? There we go!

—Pope Francis

Today, together we confirm that the Holy Rosary is not a pious practice banished to the past, like prayers of other times thought of with nostalgia. Instead, the Rosary is experiencing a new Springtime.

—Pope Benedict XVI

[The Rosary,] so easy and yet so rich, truly deserves to be rediscovered.

—Pope St. John Paul II

The Rosary is the most beautiful and the most rich in graces of all prayers; it is the prayer that touches most the Heart of the Mother of God, . . . and if you wish peace to reign in your homes, recite the family Rosary.

—Pope St. Pius X

I have said Rosaries on picket lines and in prisons, in sickness and in health, and one of our friends who lost a leg in the Second World War said that he held fast to his rosary as he lay wounded on the battlefield, holding on to it as he was hanging on to life. In peace, working for peace, suffering for peace, and suffering in war, in times of joy and pain and terror, Mary has been Refuge of Sinners.

—Dorothy Day

Where the Rosary is recited, there will be days of peace and tranquility.

—St. John Bosco

Do not be ashamed to recite the Rosary alone, while you walk along the streets to school, to the university or to work, or as you commute by public transport.

—Pope St. John Paul II

Chapter 2

SEPARATING FACT FROM MYTH

The Origins and History of the Rosary

Nothing can take the place of a good grasp of history. That goes for being a good Catholic, and it goes for being a good citizen—both of a given country and of the world—and it applies equally to being a good devotee of the Rosary. The better we understand where the Rosary came from, and the better the grasp we have of the centuries-long story of the Rosary, the greater our appreciation will be for the Rosary and for what it can do for our intimacy with Christ and for our everyday spirituality.

The origin of the Rosary is usually linked with St. Dominic de Guzmán. He lived during the twelfth and thirteenth centuries, when the Albigensian heresy was spreading across Western Europe. Albigensianism taught, among other things, that the soul is good and the body evil and that suicide is virtuous.

A lesson in the Roman Breviary—the official collection of prayers in Latin used for daily prayer by the clergy prior to Vatican II—is relevant. The breviary lesson for the feast of the Holy Rosary stated that St. Dominic de Guzmán prayed earnestly to the Blessed Virgin Mary for her assistance in combatting

Albigensianism. Mary's response, according to the legend, was to instruct St. Dominic to preach and promote the use of the Rosary as an antidote to heresy and sin.

As the story goes, the Blessed Virgin gave Dominic the Rosary and told him that if he promoted the devotion, his religious order would flourish. According to the breviary, from then on the Rosary was "most wonderfully published abroad and developed by St. Dominic, whom different Supreme Pontiffs have in various past ages of their apostolic letters declared to be the institutor and author of the same devotion."[3]

Many popes encouraged and promoted the Rosary. Indeed, they took for granted that the story about St. Dominic was historical; it actually happened. Later research has, however, led the great majority of historians and theologians to conclude that St. Dominic had nothing to do with the origins of the Rosary. Still, the occasional student or scholar of the Rosary continues to insist on the historicity of the legend, even with no scientific historical data upon which to base his or her pious opinion.

Prayers Count

In its history of the Rosary, the *Catholic Encyclopedia* notes that many religious traditions use a string of beads or some similar method to count prayers. For instance, archaeologists excavating ancient Nineveh found a sculpture of two winged female figures before a sacred tree, in a posture of prayer; each figure holds her right hand up, while in her left hand, each holds a circular string of beads.

In addition, Islam has a centuries-old tradition of using the Tasbih, or bead-string, consisting of thirty-three, sixty-six, or ninety-nine beads for counting the names of Allah. And Marco Polo, in the thirteenth century, visited a region of southern India called Malabar and reported that, to his surprise, the king there used a rosary of more than a hundred precious stones to count his prayers. In the mid-sixteenth century, St. Francis Xavier and his companions were equally astonished to find that strings of prayer beads were common among the Buddhists of Japan.

In Eastern Christianity too, rosaries have been employed for many centuries as aids to prayer. The *Catholic Encyclopedia* reports that the monks of the Greek Orthodox Church used the *kombologion* or *komboschoinion*, a cord with a hundred knots in it, to count the making of genuflections and signs of the cross. In a similar vein, buried with the mummy of a Christian ascetic named Thaias, who lived during the fourth century, archaeologists found a cribbage-board-like device, which they concluded—from accounts left by ancient authorities—was used to count prayers.

Other ancient sources report that a fourth-century hermit named, appropriately enough, Paul the Hermit took upon himself the discipline of repeating three hundred prayers every day. To keep count, he gathered up three hundred pebbles and set one aside as he completed each prayer. In the eighth century, as an act of thanksgiving for the generosity of Pope Hadrian I, the monks of St. Apollinaris were required by the pope to say *Kyrie eleison* (Lord, have mercy) three hundred times twice a day, and scholars believe that the monks must have had some way to count these prayers, perhaps using pebbles in the style of Paul the Hermit.

Scholars also discovered that as early as AD 800, all the priests in a monastery were required to say one Mass and fifty psalms for each deceased monk. Other ancient sources reveal that each monk was to sing two sets of fifty psalms for the souls of certain generous benefactors, that each priest was to sing two Masses, and that each deacon was to read two passion narratives from the Gospels.

As time went by, however, since most of the lay brothers in monasteries were illiterate and became distinct from the choir monks, they were allowed to substitute simple prayers in place of psalms. Thus, from a source dated AD 1096, we learn that when the death of a monk in another monastery was announced, every priest was to offer Mass, and every non-priest was to either say fifty psalms or repeat the Our Father fifty times.

In a similar vein, members of the Knights Templar, who followed a rule that originated in 1128, were instructed that if they could not attend choir, they were to say the Our Father fifty-seven times. And when a brother died, each monk was required to say the Our Father a hundred times a day for a week.

Obviously, with all these prayers of specific numbers being prayed, it was necessary to have some way to keep count accurately. By the eleventh and twelfth centuries, it had become common practice to use pebbles, berries, or discs of bone threaded on a string. About the year 1075, Countess Godiva of Coventry bequeathed in her will to a statue of the Blessed Virgin a circlet of precious stones that she had threaded on a string in order to keep accurate count of her prayers.

In another case, researchers found in the tomb of St. Rosalia, who died in 1160, a string of beads similar to the one mentioned by Countess Godiva. Indeed, the evidence is overwhelming that such strings of beads were common as prayer aids throughout the Middle Ages. In some European languages, these strings of beads were known as "paternosters," since *pater noster* is Latin for "Our Father." The people who made paternosters belonged to a prominent craft guild. A street in central London called Paternoster Row traces its name to the street where members of this guild gathered.[4]

It's reasonable to assume that the original purpose of these strings of beads was to count the numbers of times one recited the Our Father. This is likely not only because of their name, "paternosters," but also because the prayer we know as the Hail Mary wasn't used as a devotional prayer until the middle of the twelfth century. Sr. Shawn Madigan, CSJ, in her essay on the Rosary in *The New Dictionary of Catholic Spirituality*, notes, "Beda [bead] in medieval English means 'prayer.'"[5]

Also, she adds that in the fifteenth century, the Carthusian monk Henry of Kalkar organized the beads into sets of ten, making decades separated by a single larger bead. Thus came into being the form of rosary that remains the most common in use down to the present day.

Hail, Mary

When the Hail Mary came into popular use, it included only the first two lines of the prayer as we know it: "Hail Mary, full of grace, the Lord is with thee; blessed art thou among women, and blessed is the fruit of thy womb, Jesus." These were based on the words of the angel Gabriel and of Elizabeth to Mary in Luke 1:28, 42. Evidently, people considered these a salutation, or greeting, to Mary rather than a prayer per se, and this inspired the custom of repeating it many times in succession, often accompanied by genuflections, bows, or some other bodily act of devotion.

Generically, we might compare this practice to secular customs such as the firing of twenty-one-gun salutes by the military; applause (as we've already seen, the repetitive clapping together of the hands); or a series of cheers—("three cheers," for example)—given to honor someone. Similarly, the degree of honor given by the repetition of a prayer was measured by the number of times it was recited.

In the twelfth century, prior to the birth of St. Dominic in 1170, the custom had already become widespread of reciting 50 or 150 Hail Marys (the same number as the number of psalms in the Bible). There were many different versions of the Rosary, some using as few as five mysteries, others as many as two hundred mysteries. Only in 1569 did a Rosary utilizing fifteen mysteries—joyful, sorrowful, and glorious— become the standard, with the publication of an encyclical by Pope Pius V in which he declared that this would henceforth be the official, Church-authorized version. It would be more than four hundred years before another pontiff, Pope St. John Paul II, would add the five luminous mysteries to the Rosary.

Scholars deciphered the historical development of the Rosary from evidence present in many devotional works. In particular, one mid-twelfth-century manuscript includes instructions for how to pray fifty Hail Marys, divided into sets of ten. Similar instructions occur in a document written for a community of English hermits and dated some twenty years prior to the first Dominican foundations in that country. In other words, the custom of praying 50 or 150 Hail Marys developed apart from and prior to the preaching of St. Dominic.

Similarly remarkable is the historically verified fact that the practice of meditating on mysteries from the Gospels—in truth, the heart of the Rosary as we know it—became customary only long after the death of St. Dominic in 1221. In fact, the introduction of this practice into the Rosary was the work of a Carthusian monk, Dominic the Prussian, in the early fifteenth century. By the end of the fifteenth century, a wide variety of methods existed for praying the Rosary. The fifteen joyful, sorrowful, and glorious mysteries, which came into popular use later on, were not used even by the Dominicans.

In its article "The Rosary since Vatican II," *The Marian Library Newsletter* points out that the form of the Rosary most familiar today developed in Carthusian monasteries during the fourteenth and fifteenth centuries. As the Carthusians prayed it, the Rosary consisted of the scriptural words of the Hail Mary, with 50 and then 150 *clausulae*, or brief phrases, added after the name of Jesus: ". . . and blessed is the fruit of thy womb, Jesus." The *clausulae* evolved into the fifteen joyful, sorrowful, and glorious mysteries mentioned at the beginning of each set of ten Hail Marys.

During the Middle Ages, the second part of the Hail Mary took different forms. The wording that is so familiar today ("Holy Mary, Mother of God, pray for us sinners now and at the hour of our death. Amen.") seems to have appeared in print for the first time in the Roman Breviary published in 1568. Nothing connected this wording with the Rosary specifically, however.

The newsletter continues, saying that from this time on, because various indulgences were attached to the Rosary, its basic form remained unchanged for more than four centuries. That's because any prayer that could earn indulgences was to be said only according to a clearly prescribed form. Even perfectly admirable customs, such as the use of the *clausulae*, were forbidden—unless, of course, an exception was granted, as was in fact done for areas where German was spoken and where the *clausulae* were usually added.

We have empirical historical evidence that St. Dominic had nothing to do with originating the use of a string of beads as a counting device; nor did he think up the custom of repeating 50 or 150 Hail Marys. Both practices were in use long before Dominic was born. There is firm evidence that the practice of meditating on the mysteries came into vogue only after Dominic had been dead for two hundred years. Not even the earliest biographies of St. Dominic make any connection between the saint and the Rosary. Nor do any of the early constitutions written for the provinces of the Dominican order say anything about the Rosary.

Finally, historians located hundreds, probably thousands, of devotional writings, sermons, and other documents written by Dominican friars between 1220 and 1450—roughly the 250 years following the death of St. Dominic—and not even one mentions the Rosary. No connection appears in paintings and sculptures of the saint from these two and a half centuries. The tomb of St. Dominic in Bologna, Italy, ignores the Rosary, as do, without exception, the countless frescoes by Fra Angelico with images of Dominican friars.

Dominican Promotions

Given all this evidence, then, where did the tradition that connected the origins of the Rosary to St. Dominic come from? The *Catholic Encyclopedia* reports that all the clues historians discovered point to one source—namely, the preaching of a Dominican friar named Alanus de Rupe in the fifteenth century. He was the first to suggest that the devotion of Our Lady's Psalter, that is, the praying of 150 Hail Marys, came from or was rediscovered by St. Dominic.

Born about 1428 in Brittany, Alanus de Rupe died at Zwolle, Holland, in 1475. Early in life, he entered the Dominican order, and while pursuing his studies at St. Jacques, Paris, he distinguished himself in philosophy and theology. From 1459 to 1475, he taught almost uninterruptedly in France, Belgium, and then Rostock, Germany, where in 1473 he was made master of sacred theology. During his sixteen years of teaching, he became a renowned and popular preacher.

Alanus de Rupe seems to have been a devout, devoted, and sincere man, but evidently, as the *Catholic Encyclopedia* suggests, he was also somewhat deluded. He based his claims about the Rosary and St. Dominic upon the testimony of writers who never existed. All the same, the Rosary confraternities organized by de Rupe and his confreres in cities such as Douai and Cologne attracted a great many enthusiastic participants. Following his death, numerous books were published that were filled with the ideas of Alanus de Rupe.

This, then, is the source of the legend that St. Dominic received the Rosary from the Blessed Virgin Mary. Pope Leo X was the first pope to write approvingly of this legend, as though it might be factual, in 1520, but he did so with some reserve. Many later popes, however, accepted the legend as historical, with few if any reservations at all.

There is no doubt, of course, that the widespread popularity of the Rosary in the modern era and the immeasurable good that has come from it are due in large part to the efforts and prayers of Dominican friars and women religious. But the historical evidence leaves no doubt that Dominican interest in the Rosary emerged only during the last years of the fifteenth century, long after the death of St. Dominic.

A Circle of Roses

As far as the name "Rosary" is concerned, it comes from the Latin word *rosarius*, meaning a garland or bouquet of roses. The earliest use of the term was figurative as, for example, in the title of a book to refer to a collection of short writings or selections from longer works. A widely popular medieval European legend told a story in which the Blessed Virgin Mary took rosebuds from the lips of a young monk as he recited Hail Marys. She then wove the rosebuds into a garland, which she placed upon her own head.

The name "Our Lady's Psalter," perhaps the first name given to what we know as the Rosary, dates to about the same era. In the fourteenth-century works of Chaucer, the old English name was a "pair of beads," the word "bead" originally meaning "prayers."

The Rosary, in various forms, has been a popular part of Catholic devotional spirituality for nearly seven hundred years. *The Marian Library Newsletter* reports that Pope Leo

XIII (1878–1903) wrote no fewer than thirteen encyclicals on the Rosary, and in the twentieth century, popes have time and again encouraged its use. Pope St. John Paul II, whose papacy linked the twentieth and twenty-first centuries, promoted the Rosary as much as anyone.

During the twentieth century, countless ordinary Catholics, priests, bishops, men and women religious, and notable Catholic intellectuals—the great German Jesuit theologian Karl Rahner, the American Trappist monk and author Thomas Merton, and Dorothy Day, the cofounder of the Catholic Worker movement, among them—prayed the Rosary regularly.

In the 1940s, '50s, and early '60s, Rosary devotions, crusades, and football-stadium-size rallies were popular parts of Catholic life. Messages from the Marian apparitions at Fátima and Lourdes included calls to pray the Rosary. The popular American "television priest," Bishop Fulton Sheen, explained the use of the Rosary to huge audiences, both Catholic and non-Catholic. Fr. Patrick Peyton, of the Congregation of Holy Cross, the famous "Rosary priest," worked unceasingly to promote the Rosary through crusades and rallies in many parts of the world.

Crisis and Restoration

In the mid-1960s, the Second Vatican Council recommended devotion to Mary but said nothing about the Rosary. The council rightly placed considerable emphasis on the centrality of the Mass in Catholic life. Following Vatican II, evening Masses replaced evening Marian devotions in some places, and the assumption became widespread that participation in the Mass ought to take the place of all communal and private devotions. However, there is no evidence that Vatican II meant to do away with popular devotions such as the Rosary. All the council did was teach that popular devotions should not compete with the Eucharist but should support and lead to it.

All the same, during the decades following the Second Vatican Council, the Rosary was far less in evidence than it had been during the first half of the twentieth century. During the 1970s, what some perceived to be a crisis in Marian devotion was well under way. Some charged that both Vatican II and the liturgical reforms sparked by the council were deeply anti-Marian. In May 1971, Fr. Patrick Peyton, director of the Family Rosary Crusade, wrote a strongly worded letter to Pope Paul VI, in which he urged the pope to declare the Rosary a liturgical prayer. This would have placed it on the same level as, for example, the Liturgy of the Hours, formerly known as the Roman Breviary.

Pope Paul VI asked the Vatican Congregation for Divine Worship to prepare a draft of a document that would encourage families to pray the Rosary. The members of the congregation asked Fr. Ignacio Calabuig, OSM, and the faculty of the Pontifical Theological Faculty Marianum, in Rome, to study the matter and compose a draft for an encyclical. Three years and four revisions later, the faculty sent a draft to the pope, including three forms of the Rosary the pope might recommend. Pope Paul VI responded to this suggestion with disapproval, noting that it would be confusing and discouraging to people to appear to alter the traditional form of the Rosary.

Marialis Cultus (For the Right Ordering and Development of Devotion to the Blessed Virgin Mary), the apostolic exhortation by Pope Paul VI on devotion to Mary, originally inspired by Fr. Peyton's 1971 letter, was published in February 1974. The document discussed the place of Marian devotion in the liturgy of the Church, provided directives for developing that devotion, and encouraged the restoration and a better understanding of the Rosary among the people. It also included a section outlining the characteristics of the Rosary, which *The Marian Library Newsletter* summarizes succinctly in these words:

> Contemplative—"By its nature . . . the Rosary calls for a quiet rhythm and a lingering pace, helping the individual to meditate on the mysteries of the Lord's life as seen through the eyes of her who was closest to the Lord." Without the contemplative element, the Rosary becomes a "mechanical repetition of formulas, . . . a body without a soul."
>
> Christ-centered and Marian—"The Rosary is a 'compendium of the entire Gospel,' . . . centered on the mystery of the redemptive Incarnation." It is directed toward the events of Christ's life as seen by Mary.
>
> In Harmony with the Liturgy—Since the Rosary is centered on the mysteries celebrated in the liturgy, it is "excellent preparation" for and a "continuing echo" of the liturgy.[6]

The newsletter goes on to say that *Marialis Cultus* also called for adaptations to the Rosary so that its "spiritual richness" might be appreciated more.

Praying with Mary

The widespread popularity of the Rosary down through the centuries should not be taken to mean, however, that it suited everyone equally. *The Marian Library Newsletter* notes that in her writings, the great nineteenth-century French mystic and saint Thérèse of Lisieux wrote words that, in the first editions of the manuscript that later became her autobiography, were deleted by well-meaning editors. Thérèse wrote, "What difficulties I have had throughout my life with saying the Rosary. I am ashamed to say that the recitation of the Rosary was at times more painful than an instrument of torture."

The newsletter went on to point out that, in a similar vein, Fr. Vincent Dwyer, a twentieth-century American Trappist monk and author, wrote that the Rosary is "one of the great vehicles that helped people enter the quiet space with the Master." Yet, he continued, "I myself find it impossible to say the Rosary, but it is always with me in my pocket."

While the Rosary experienced some decline during the last thirty or forty years of the twentieth century, the first few years of the twenty-first century are witnessing an increase in interest in this traditional prayer form. There is something about the Rosary that makes it attractive and rewarding.

St. Thérèse and Fr. Dwyer will always have their sympathizers, and for some, the Rosary may never be suitable. But most people who give the Rosary a chance find themselves basking in its spiritual riches and in the calm that it tends to engender. The Rosary is a prayer of quiet, of listening, and of active acceptance of God's will in all things, and this kind of prayer will never be out of fashion.

The Rosary, as we know it today, is the result of a centuries-long development. Still, the heart of the matter has always been basically the same. Praying the Rosary is a way for devout, faith-filled Catholics to remind themselves that "this is the day that the LORD has made" (Psalm 118:24). Above all, the Rosary is a way to bring to mind the life and gospel of Christ in companionship with his—and our—Blessed Mother, Mary.

CHAPTER 3

MORE THAN JUST A STRING
OF BEADS

The Prayers of the Rosary

Each of the prayers that makes up the Rosary contributes something essential to a balanced, mature Christian faith and to adult ways of living that faith. We can say, indeed, that the Rosary reflects the most basic aspects of the Christian faith. Let's take a look at these prayers and see what we can gain toward a deeper understanding of each one.

The Sign of the Cross

> In the name of the Father, and of the Son, and of the Holy Spirit. Amen.

The Rosary begins with the Sign of the Cross, which gives the entire Rosary a trinitarian character, invoking the triune God: Father, Son, and Holy Spirit. With this prayer and its accompanying sacred gesture—touching forehead, then chest, then left and right shoulders—we also declare our commitment to the Catholic faith and the one, holy, catholic, and apostolic Church, whose mission it is to live, nourish, and preserve that faith in this world. We do not pray only in the name of the Father, or only in the name of the Son, or only in the name of the Holy Spirit, but in the name of the triune God.

By this prayer-gesture, we remind ourselves, too, that we do all things in the name of the cross of Christ. We remind ourselves of the cross not merely as the instrument of the death of Jesus more than two thousand years ago, but as the means of our salvation. By virtue of our baptism, all the dark, painful, troubled, and anguished times in our lives become a share in the cross of Christ, through which we will also share in his resurrection. We affirm our acceptance of this reality when we bless ourselves with the Sign of the Cross.

At the same time, by making the Sign of the Cross, we affirm our identity as Catholics, for one of the ancient traditions that the Protestant Reformation abandoned was this one. Indeed, we have written testimony from the early second century that Christians practiced the custom of tracing the Sign of the Cross on their foreheads. So for many generations up to the present day, to bless oneself with the Sign of the Cross has been to identify oneself as Catholic. The Eastern Orthodox churches retain this tradition too but in a slightly different form, touching the right shoulder first and then the left.

Making the Sign of the Cross, we pray, saying, "In the name of the Father, and of the Son, and of the Holy Spirit." But what, we may ask, does it mean to pray "in the name of" someone? In ordinary human parlance, to speak in someone else's name means to speak for him or her, to represent his or her thoughts and, indeed, his or her person. An attorney speaks "in the name of" the client, for example. A diplomatic envoy speaks "in the name of" the president or government of his or her country. In other words, to speak "in the name of" someone else is to present oneself as a genuinely designated representative of that other person and as one appointed to speak for him or her.

It may seem presumptuous, therefore, to pray "in the name of" the Father, the Son, and the Holy Spirit. By what right do we address our prayers to the triune God "in the name of" the Trinity's own self? But that is the great joy and dignity of our baptism. For when we were baptized, we were baptized into Christ, and we were baptized "in the name of the Father, and of the Son, and of the Holy Spirit." Through baptism we became members of the mystical body of Christ. As St. Paul explains, "Now you are the body of Christ and individually members of it" (1 Corinthians 12:27).

So to prayerfully make the Sign of the Cross and speak the words "In the name of the Father, and of the Son, and of the Holy Spirit" is to speak from our membership in the body of Christ that St. Paul talks about. Because we are "in Christ," there is no distance between God and us, and we can pray to God in his own name. When the Father looks at his Son, we might say, he cannot help but see us too.

The Apostles' Creed

I believe in God, the Father almighty, Creator of heaven and earth, and in Jesus Christ, his only Son, our Lord, who was conceived by the Holy Spirit, born of the Virgin Mary, suffered under Pontius Pilate, was crucified, died and was buried; he descended into hell; on the third day he rose again from the dead; he ascended into heaven, and is seated at the right hand of God the Father almighty; from there he will come to judge the living and the dead. I believe in the Holy Spirit, the holy catholic Church, the communion of saints, the forgiveness of sins, the resurrection of the body, and life everlasting. Amen.

Although the Apostles' Creed didn't become part of the Rosary until sometime in the seventeenth century, it is the oldest extant prayer of its kind in the Christian tradition, dating back to the early decades of the Church. It was not, however, as the title may suggest, composed by the twelve apostles of Jesus. Rather, the point of this title is that the prayer conveys the "mind" of the apostles—the content of their belief, if you will.

When we pray the Apostles' Creed, we consciously unite ourselves to the earliest followers of the risen Christ and to the countless ordinary believers—saints and sinners—who preceded us down through history, endless numbers of whom prayed the very prayer we pray and held in their hands rosaries very much like the rosaries we hold in our hands today as we say this prayer.

The words of this creed, this prayerful, concise expression of the content of our belief, carry considerable meaning in every phrase, so we will benefit from taking a closer look at each part of the prayer.

"*I believe in God, the Father almighty, . . .*" With these words, we embrace the metaphor for God clearly preferred by Jesus in the Gospels and, indeed, by the New Testament as a whole— namely, "Father." The Aramaic word that Jesus used is *Abba*, which is perhaps more accurately translated as "Papa" or even "loving Papa." This, at any rate, is how we should understand the metaphor *Father* when applied to God. In other words, metaphorically speaking, God has the same warm, strong, welcoming, and always-forgiving love for us that a human "loving papa" has for his children. More about the term *Father* in the section on the Our Father.

To "Father," the creed immediately adds the modifier "almighty." A dictionary defines *almighty* as "having absolute power; all-powerful." Sometimes we wonder why, if God is almighty, he doesn't do something to stop the wars, innocent suffering, and cruelty in the world. Why doesn't God simply rid the world of evil? Why doesn't God cure people who have terminal illnesses? Why doesn't he punish people who hurt innocent children? To ask such questions, however, is to misunderstand who God is and in what sense he is almighty.

God's all-powerfulness is absolute, but so also is his wisdom, which leaves all human beings free—free even to choose evil and act maliciously. And while terminal illnesses, natural disasters, and the like wreak havoc and spread pain and sorrow, all these things provide us with opportunities to practice charity and act in "God-like" ways, if we will, toward one another. Our belief in an all-powerful God leaves both the mystery of God's love and the reality of evil and suffering intact.

The almightiness of God is best understood in his action as Creator, as the source of all things in creation; hence, the words that immediately follow *almighty.* Also, it is no accident that the Apostles' Creed calls God "almighty" and "Father"— that is, "loving Papa"—at the same time. The two images are meant to condition and qualify each other. It makes perfect sense, then, that this prayer is followed immediately by the prayer that addresses God as "our Father."

"... *Creator of heaven and earth,* ..." So the God who is both "almighty" and "Father" (loving Papa) is precisely the God who created or brought into existence everything that is. He created the world "according to his wisdom," not because he needed to or by chance, but because he "wanted to make his creatures share in his being, wisdom, and goodness" (CCC 295). God had no other reason for creating us other than his love and goodness, and he wants to share his life with us, his creatures.

"... *and [I believe] in Jesus Christ, his only Son, our Lord,* ..." These words make the point that Jesus of Nazareth, who became the risen Christ, is the "only" Son of God. Here is the second real crunch point of the Apostles' Creed. The first one is belief in God. Given belief in God, however, once you believe that Jesus is and was God's "only Son," then you have no choice but to be a Christian. No other major religious founder, leader, or prophet has ever claimed to be who Jesus and the Christian tradition claim that he is—namely, God's "only Son." If you believe this, then the only intellectually honest choice you can make is to be a Christian.

"... *who was conceived by the Holy Spirit, born of the Virgin Mary, suffered under Pontius Pilate, was crucified, died and was buried* ..." The main point of these words is to declare Jesus' divine and human nature and the truth that he really and truly lived and died in a specific time and place in actual human history. "Why mention Pontius Pilate?" one might ask. The point of mentioning the name of the Roman figure most directly responsible for Jesus' crucifixion is to emphasize the historicity of Jesus' life and death, to fix it at a precise time in human history—namely, during the years when the Roman procurator of Judea was one Pontius Pilate, from about the years AD 25 to 35. The main point of these words is to declare that Jesus, in both his humanity and his divinity, endured the pain of being nailed to a cross and died a real death, and his really and truly dead body was placed in a tomb.

" . . . *he descended into hell* . . . " Probably the most perplexing words in the Apostles' Creed, this phrase may leave even many Catholics wondering what it means. However, a few minutes of research clear things up considerably.

In his still excellent work *Dictionary of the Bible,* the late Fr. John L. McKenzie is about as helpful as anyone has ever been or is ever likely to be when it comes to explaining the point of this phrase. Fr. McKenzie writes,

> The phrase "descended into hell" rests upon the language of the OT [Old Testament]. "Hell" here represents the Hb [Hebrew] Sheol, the abode of the dead. The concept of Sheol in the OT implies no reward or punishment and no distinction between the state of the good and the wicked. In the OT "to die" is "to descend into Sheol" and one who rises from the dead rises from Sheol.[7]

In other words, the Apostles' Creed is redundant here. It says something like, "He died, and he really and truly died." Interpretations of this phrase that rely upon legendary traditions—suggesting, for example, that when Jesus died, he went to release from hell the great figures from the Old Testament era—are best ignored. As Father McKenzie comments, such interpretations "have no basis in the NT [New Testament]."

" . . . *on the third day he rose again from the dead . . .* "
With the statement that Jesus' resurrection happened on "the
third day," once again the Apostles' Creed insists on the tem-
poral and historical nature of events that is foundational to
the Christian faith and to the Church. Then, with no attempt
to interpret or explain, the creed simply states the resurrection of Jesus as a historical fact. Those who have experienced
the presence of the risen Lord need no proof, and for those who
have not, no proof is possible.

Empirical, scientific data are not the only valid and accept-
able kinds of data upon which to base one's life, choices, and
behavior. In other words, even atheism is as much of a belief
system as any religion, requiring a similar "leap of faith."
(Indeed, what else but a kind of "faith" could support the athe-
ist's irrational belief that something can come from nothing?)

These words do not attempt to explain Jesus' resurrection;
they leave the mystery intact. Theologians may ponder and
hypothesize, and they may do so to our benefit. Indeed, some
suggest, for example, that Jesus' resurrection was an event that
happened in, but also transcended, time and space. Such attempts
to aid the modern imagination can be helpful, but none will ever
clear up the ultimate mystery of the Christian faith. The believing "heart" relates better to the resurrection than does the intellect, but it can never be divorced from the intellect.

" . . . *he ascended into heaven, and is seated at the right hand
of God the Father almighty . . .* " These words clarify metaphorically that through his resurrection, Jesus entered, fully
human and fully divine, into complete intimacy with the same
Father first named in the beginning of the creed.

" . . . *from there he will come to judge the living and the dead.*" This phrase echoes the words of Jesus in Matthew 25:31-46. There Jesus tells the familiar story of the sheep and goats at the last judgment. The inclination may be to place the emphasis on the judgment, but the clear intention of Jesus in telling this story is to teach his disciples the importance of feeding the hungry, clothing the naked, and so forth.

So fundamental are these works of mercy that our eternal destiny depends on whether we act in merciful ways toward others or not. That's probably the best idea to keep in mind with regard to the words in the Apostles' Creed regarding the final judgment too. The intention is not to scare the living daylights out of us but to inspire us to live and act in compassionate ways.

"*I believe in the Holy Spirit, . . .*" With the first two Persons of the Holy Trinity already covered earlier in the prayer, the creed now makes clear that Christians do believe in a triune God, the third Person of whom is the Holy Spirit. The creed declares belief in the Spirit without attempting to provide a theological explanation of the Holy Spirit's identity. That was left to later theological reflection. All that matters here is that Christian faith includes belief in Father, Son, and Holy Spirit. One must look elsewhere to clarify the nature of belief in the Trinity.

" . . . *the holy catholic Church, . . .*" The *Catechism of the Catholic Church* explains that the lowercase "c" for the word *catholic* in this phrase means "universal," in the sense of "according to the totality" or "in keeping with the whole." "The Church is catholic in a double sense," the *Catechism* adds. First, "Christ is present in her." The Church was catholic on the day of Pentecost and will always be so until the day of the Second Coming. And second, "she has been sent out by Christ on a mission to the whole of the human race" (CCC 830, 831). Everyone is called to belong to the People of God, and no one is excluded.

" . . . *the communion of saints, . . .* " This is one of the least-appreciated aspects of Catholic belief. In truth, this belief encompasses so much as to boggle the mind. In a nutshell, as we noted earlier, "the communion of saints" refers to the entire community that is the Church, in time and space and eternity. Everyone who belongs to the Church now present in the world and in history and everyone who ever belonged to the Church and has "passed on" to the mystery that is eternity in heaven belong to the communion of saints.

In the creed, we express our belief that we belong to a community that is in, and transcends, the everyday world we experienced yesterday, are experiencing today, and will probably experience tomorrow. The mind-boggling part happens when we begin to ponder the implications of our membership in this community. If all this is true, what does it mean here and now?

This isn't the appropriate place to go into all the possibilities—that could take another book. But think it over. What does it mean to you that you have a real and intimate personal relationship with all other believers in the world and with all those who have already passed through the thin veil that separates this world from the next?

" . . . *the forgiveness of sins, . . .* " Well, you may think, this isn't so difficult to understand. We believe that God forgives sins, of course. Nothing complicated about that. Ah, but believing in the forgiveness of sins in the abstract is one thing, and believing in the forgiveness of sins for, say, yourself is quite another.

You there—you with all your mostly pitiful little sins, and your mean, selfish little sinfulness, and your huge tendency to not really trust in God's love—you there, do you really and truly believe in the forgiveness of your sins? Or do you have sins that you just can't forget about, even if you have already confessed them in the Sacrament of Reconciliation? If so, chances are that you have a tough time believing in the forgiveness of sins. Psychological insights into spirituality insist that sometimes the most difficult part of believing in God's forgiveness is being able to forgive yourself. So this isn't as simple as it looks, is it?

"*. . . the resurrection of the body, . . .*" We rattle this phrase off easily; how smoothly it rolls off the tongue. Here it is, what we might call the ultimate mystery of the Christian life, and with a blithe spirit we claim it for ourselves. It is a "mystery," we admit that. But do we realize that for Christian faith, a mystery isn't the same thing as a nut to crack or a puzzle to solve?

Theologians try at length to explain the meaning of Christian mysteries. Certainly the kind of mystery that faith speaks of isn't the same as the kinds of mysteries you find in "whodunit" novels. A Christian mystery isn't merely something that we'll never completely understand, although it is that too. Also, a Christian mystery isn't just a truth that we can only accept because it is revealed by God.

Perhaps the best and most concise way to explain what we mean by "mystery" here is that it is a human experience of the divine; we can experience it, but we can't fully grasp it intellectually. The heart can know it better than the intellect can know it, although the intellect can know something *about* it. We need to be able to trust both brain and heart. Authentic Christian faith includes both the mind and the heart, and we have a tendency to trust one more than the other, when we need to trust both. Well might we reflect on the admonition of the seventeenth-century French Catholic mathematician and philosopher Blaise Pascal, who understood the need to balance both intellect and heart. "If we submit everything to reason," he wrote, "our religion will be left with nothing mysterious or supernatural. If we offend the principles of reason, our religion will be absurd and ridiculous."[8]

The point here is that the resurrection is the ultimate mystery for any of us, because when we pray the Apostles' Creed, we claim that we accept the fact that our ultimate destiny is "the resurrection of the body." The best, indeed the only, information we have about what this means comes from the resurrection narratives in the Gospels, especially the accounts of the disciples' encounters with the risen Jesus. From these narratives, we gather more about what resurrection does not mean than what it does mean.

Resurrection does not mean the resuscitation of a corpse, for it's clear that the risen Christ's body is not the same as your run-of-the-mill, everyday body. He enters rooms without using the door, for example. Yet he shares a meal of cooked fish, and he invites Thomas to touch his wounds, so we're not talking about a totally spiritualized, nonmaterial body either.

The long and the short of it is that, first, we believe that our ultimate destiny includes "the resurrection of the body." And second, we sure look forward to experiencing that, whatever it is!

"*. . . and life everlasting. Amen.*" This final phrase from the Apostles' Creed can be misleading, because "everlasting" is a concept that relies on categories of time and space. "Everlasting" sounds like endless time, but that's not what the creed means here. It means "eternal" life, and "eternal" is not the same as "everlasting." The reference here is to what we might call another way, or mode, of being—and even that doesn't do it justice. The point is that we pass through ordinary death to Something Else and We're Really Going to Like It. And we'll find out what it is only on the other side of death.

The final word, "Amen," means, of course, that we totally agree with and embrace everything we just said in praying the Apostles' Creed—or at least, we want to totally embrace it, and we're trying to totally embrace it. "Lord, I do believe; help my unbelief" (cf. Mark 9:24). It's a sort of religious term for "Right on!" or "Ain't no doubt about it!"

The Our Father

The Our Father is based upon the prayer Jesus teaches his disciples in the Gospels of Matthew (6:9-13) and Luke (11:2-4), more the former than the latter. This is the one prayer that all Christians share, for precisely this reason, although Protestants add an ancient doxology, "For thine is the kingdom, and the power, and the glory, forever and ever." Because this doxology is not without historical merit today, Catholics add a version of it in the context of the Mass only, separated from the Our Father itself by a prayer said by the priest.

Jesus teaches his disciples to address God as *Abba* ("Father" or "loving Papa"). Christian feminists occasionally suggest that sometimes we should also use the metaphor "Mother" to refer to God. They base this suggestion on the assertion that to use the metaphor "Father" for God, or to use masculine pronouns to refer to God, supports and fosters authoritarian paternalism and anti-female biases in the Church. This assertion can be neither proven nor disproven.

Regardless of the cultural or theological ideologies of our particular historical era, however, there are compelling historical, scriptural, and practical reasons to continue using for God the metaphorical appellation "Father" and the masculine pronouns consistent with it.

It's true that, in a few instances in the Gospels, Jesus uses a female character as a metaphor for God, such as the woman who lights a candle and sweeps her house searching for a lost silver coin, in Luke 15:8-10. In Matthew 23:37, Jesus compares himself to the hen who gathers her brood under her wings. But Jesus never calls God his or our "mother," and he never uses feminine pronouns to refer directly to God. Rather, the only mother Jesus has is his human mother, Mary. By extension, in virtue of our baptism, we must say the same. In Christ, God is our Father, and Mary is our mother—God in divine, loving, papa-like ways, Mary in heavenly yet human, mother-like ways—always keeping in mind the special nature of her relationship with her fully divine and fully human Son.

In his book *Calling God "Father": Essays on the Bible, Fatherhood & Culture*, Canadian Protestant Scripture scholar John W. Miller writes,

Not once in biblical tradition is God ever spoken of as "she" or "her" or regarded as genderless. On the other hand, God is not portrayed there simply as male either, but as a father whose tenderness and compassion are often mother-like. In no instance does this imply that God has become a mother-figure to his worshipers. The uniformity of the canonical representation of God as father is one of its most notable features.[9]

That said, we must note that gender is a human characteristic. It is a divine characteristic only metaphorically. But for Jesus to become human, he had to be born of a woman. From a human perspective, then, and consistent with the way that we as human beings understand procreation, Mary is Jesus' mother, and God is Jesus' father. In calling God his and our Father a relationship with which we, as human beings, are intimately familiar, Jesus tells us a great deal, not only about how we should relate to God, but about how God relates to us. That is not to say that God isn't mother-like as well as father-like but that, from a human standpoint, it wouldn't make sense to call God "Mother."

Some Catholic feminists, in liturgical references and elsewhere, change references to God as "Father" to "God," thus substituting an impersonal, genderless God for a personal, fatherly God. Sometimes they change "Father" to "Mother." In other instances, they change "Father" to "loving God" or "compassionate God." Such changes, though, while well intentioned, are inconsistent with scriptural tradition and with our understanding of familial relationships.

At the same time, however, we must admit that the version of the Our Father used most commonly includes words and phrases that are either archaic, misleading, or both. This familiar version is beloved by the countless people who use it, and it is highly unlikely that it will be changed in the foreseeable future. Still, for the sake of a better understanding of the Our Father, it can be helpful to look at the meanings most likely first intended both by Jesus and by Matthew and Luke, who record the Our Father in their Gospels.

At first glance, the text of the Our Father in Matthew's Gospel (below, left) seems rather similar to the standard form of the Our Father (below, right). As we go line by line through the text, however, we will notice places at which Matthew's Gospel seems to better convey Jesus' meaning, particularly toward the end of the prayer:

Matthew 6:9-13	Our Father
Our Father in heaven,	Our Father, who art in heaven,
hallowed be your name.	hallowed be thy name;
Your kingdom come.	thy kingdom come;
Your will be done,	thy will be done
on earth as it	on earth as it
is in heaven.	is in heaven.
Give us this day	Give us this day
our daily bread.	our daily bread;
And forgive us our debts,	and forgive us our trespasses
as we also have forgiven	as we forgive those who
our debtors.	trespass against us;
And do not bring us to	and lead us not into
the time of trial,	temptation,
but rescue us from	but deliver us from evil.
the evil one.	Amen.

"Our Father, who art in heaven, hallowed be thy name . . . "
Jesus taught his apostles that God is our Father as well as his,
and we acknowledge that relationship when we pray this first
line. We don't talk about many things as being "hallowed"
these days, and in fact, "hallowed" is a rather old-fashioned
if not archaic word for "holy" or "sanctified." So when we
begin to say the Our Father, we acknowledge that we think of
God as a father and that he is worthy of our devotion.

". . . thy kingdom come . . . " In this line, we express our
desire to bring about the kingdom of God on earth—as he originally intended it at the creation of the world. The Greek term
basileia, translated as "kingdom" here, is sometimes also translated "reign," which suggests even more the active or dynamic
nature of what Jesus is talking about. The Greek word refers,
in essence, to the glory of God or God's very presence, permeating all of creation.

The late Fr. Raymond Brown, SS, in his pioneering essay
"The Pater Noster as an Eschatological Prayer," suggested that
if we were to paraphrase, we might say that "Thy kingdom
come" means something like "May your divine presence permeate all of creation right now."[10]

' *. . . thy will be done on earth as it is in heaven."* Jesus,
as well as the early Jewish Christian community for which
the Gospel of Matthew was written, took it for granted that
God's will refers to God's ultimate plan for all creation, that
is, the redemption and subjection of all things to the Father's
will, specifically in the person of his Son, Jesus (see Ephesians
1:5-12). When the early Christians prayed these words, they
knew full well that they were asking their Father/loving Papa

to bring about, immediately, the completion of all things in Christ and the end of time. Think about that the next time you pray these words!

"Give us this day our daily bread. . . " Who does not assume that this is a petitionary prayer for three square meals a day? While this is a perfectly understandable prayer to pray, it's not what these words mean. Fr. Brown suggests that what Jesus refers to here is the "living" bread of the Eucharist. It makes perfect sense, then that the Our Father begins the Communion Rite in the Mass.

Other scholars suggest a different interpretation, which also has its basis in Scripture. In this interpretation, when we ask God to "give us this day our daily bread," we give control of our lives completely to him and agree to follow his will for us. In the same chapter of Matthew's Gospel, Jesus says, "Do not worry, saying, 'What will we eat?' or 'What will we drink?' or 'What will we wear?' . . . Indeed your heavenly Father knows that you need all these things. But strive first for the kingdom of God and his righteousness, and all these things will be given to you as well" (6:31, 32-33).

" . . . and forgive us our trespasses as we forgive those who trespass against us . . ." The key word here is "forgive." We ask for our Father's forgiveness in light of our forgiveness of others. The Greek word translated "trespasses" in the familiar version of the prayer is, however, more accurately translated as "debts," as in the above translation of Matthew's Gospel: "And forgive us our debts, as we also have forgiven our debtors" (6:12).

The implication seems to be that sin results in being indebted. If we presume that sin damages our relationships with both God and neighbor, then through sin we become spiritually indebted to both God and neighbor. The second part of this phrase makes a direct correlation between God's forgiveness of us and our forgiveness of those whose sins leave them indebted to us. God's forgiveness of us depends on our forgiveness of one another.

"*. . . and lead us not into temptation, . . .*" If any part of the familiar version of the Our Father begs to be changed, it's probably this one, because it so clearly misrepresents the meaning intended by Jesus and by the Gospel of Matthew. The trouble with this phrase is that it implies that God is responsible for temptation. There are some ancient texts in the Old Testament that speak of God tempting people, but usually the reference is more to a testing, not to God actually trying to trip people up. The New Testament's Letter of James says, "No one, when tempted, should say, 'I am being tempted by God'; for God cannot be tempted by evil and he himself tempts no one" (1:13).

We can avoid this conundrum if, with Fr. Brown, we realize that the intended meaning of this phrase is a reference to the final conflict, at the end of time, between God and Satan. A better translation might be "and lead us not into trial" (see the text of the Our Father in Matthew's Gospel), which is actually, in the original Greek, a prayer asking God to spare us from any need to even show our faces to Satan at the final coming of the kingdom of God.

"*. . . but deliver us from evil.*" Some Scripture scholars opt for translating this "but deliver us from the evil one," as in the translation of the Our Father in Matthew's Gospel, instead of "from evil." Regardless, the meaning is clear: we are petitioning our Father to save us from all kinds of bad news and bad experiences—all that is bad, wrong, or wicked in any way.

"*Amen.*" Catholics sometimes forget to conclude the Our Father with an "amen" because they have learned not to say it at Mass until after the priest's prayer and the doxology. But as in our other prayers, it is an important sign that we believe and intend to live by the words that we have just prayed.

It seems more than fitting that the Our Father have a prominent place in the Rosary as a Christian devotional prayer because it is the prayer that Jesus taught us to pray. It is the indispensable prayer for Christians that sums up and crowns all of our prayers by affirming our relationship with God as well as the way we are to live our lives.

The Hail Mary

Hail Mary, full of grace,
the Lord is with thee/you;
blessed art thou/are you among women,
and blessed is the fruit of thy/your womb, Jesus.
Holy Mary, Mother of God, pray for us sinners
now and at the hour of our death. Amen.

The Hail Mary is recited more times in the Rosary than any other prayer, and it is the prayer that we most commonly associate with the Rosary. As we know it today, the Hail Mary consists of three sentences, two of which are scriptural greetings and the last of which is a petition. Like the Our Father, the familiar version of the Hail Mary uses the archaic words "thee," "thy," and "art thou" rather than the more contemporary if also more pedestrian terms "you," "your," and "are you." The older version of the prayer may be more poetic and may suggest more of a sense of holiness and mystery, but you should feel free to use whichever version is more comfortable for you.

"Hail Mary, full of grace, the Lord is with thee (you) . . ." When we say the first part of the Hail Mary, we echo the greeting of the angel Gabriel to Mary in the Gospel of Luke's infancy narrative. When the angel appeared to Mary, he said, "Greetings, favored one! The Lord is with you. . . . [Y]ou have found favor with God" (1:28, 30). When we greet Mary in this way, we acknowledge the special grace that God bestowed upon her in asking her to be the mother of his Son.

Alert readers will notice what may seem like a contradiction between the wording of the Hail Mary and its source in Luke 1:28. The prayer begins, "Hail Mary, full of grace." However, virtually all modern translations of Luke 1:28—including the official Catholic version, the New American Bible Revised Edition—translate the angel's words without using the word "grace" at all. Thus, in the NABRE: "Hail, favored one!"

So what's up here? After·all, "full of grace" and "favored one" seem different theologically. Indeed, "full of grace" may strike the reader as attributing to Mary greater dignity than "favored one." If Luke's Gospel actually says "favored one," what basis do we have for the Hail Mary to say "full of grace"?

Historically, the phrase "full of grace" originated with the late sixteenth-to mid-eighteenth-century Douay-Rheims Bible, an English version based on the Latin Vulgate Bible, which was translated from Hebrew and Greek manuscripts by St. Jerome (AD 342–420). The Douay-Rheims Bible, in other words, is an eighteenth-century English translation of a fifth-century Latin translation, not a translation from the original Hebrew and Greek manuscripts.

When St. Jerome translated the Greek text of Luke 1:28 into Latin, he rendered the word *kecharitōmenē* as *gratia plena,* "full of grace." Then, thirteen centuries later, the Douay-Rheims translators merely followed suit and gave *gratia plena* the literal translation, "full of grace." That's where the Hail Mary in Latin gets *gratia plena* and in English gets "full of grace."

Those who translated the Douay-Rheims Bible could have been more careful and paid closer attention to the Greek texts. Some think they were influenced more by their own Catholic theological preferences and piety than by meanings inherent in the Greek and Hebrew texts.

This is not the end of the discussion, however, for the Douay-Rheims translators' preference for "full of grace" is not without support internal to the Greek text. As we have already seen, the Greek word in Luke 1:28 translated as either "full of grace" or "favored one" is *kecharitōmenē.* While scholarly consensus seems to be that Luke intends "favored one," this is an instance where differences of opinion are important.

Notice that the word at the heart of *kecharitōmenē* is the Greek word for "grace," namely, *"charis,"* meaning God's self-gift to us. Also, the author of the commentary on the Gospel of Luke in the *New Jerome Biblical Commentary*—probably today's most prestigious Catholic Bible commentary—translates *kecharitōmenē* as "Graced One."

Note also how this Greek term is translated in the current edition of *The Book of the Gospels*—that is, the collection of Gospel readings proclaimed during the Mass' Liturgy of the Word. The editors of *The Book of the Gospels* chose to render *kecharitōmenē* in, for example, the Gospel reading for the feast of the Immaculate Conception (December 8) as "full of grace." The use in *The Book of the Gospels* of "full of grace" instead of "favored one" remains significant. Given the full meaning of *kecharitōmenē*, as well as the extensive history and tradition of translating this word as "full of grace," we may certainly continue to pray, "Hail Mary, full of grace."

" . . . *blessed art thou (are you) among women, and blessed is the fruit of thy (your) womb, Jesus.*" Up until the name "Jesus," these are the words that Mary's relative Elizabeth speaks to her upon her arrival (see Luke 1:42). In using this greeting and adding Jesus' name, we share Elizabeth's excitement that God's plan of salvation is unfolding through Mary, and we recognize—along with Elizabeth—that Mary is indeed the mother of our Lord.

"*Holy Mary, Mother of God, pray for us sinners now and at the hour of our death. Amen.*" This last line is the actual prayer, or petition, of the Hail Mary, which didn't officially become part of the prayer until sometime in the sixteenth century. Individuals occasionally added their own similar supplications, such as this one from the fourteenth century, which the *Catholic Encyclopedia* notes has been incorrectly attributed to Dante: "Oh Blessed Virgin, pray to God for us always, that he may pardon us and give us grace, so to live here below that he may reward us with paradise at our death."[11]

The form of the prayer that we use today was included in the Roman Breviary in 1568. The *Catechism of the Council of Trent* attributed the addition of that final line to the Church itself, writing,

Most rightly has the Holy Church of God added to this thanksgiving, petition also, and the invocation of the most holy Mother of God, thereby implying that we should piously and suppliantly have recourse to her in order that by her intercession she may reconcile God with us sinners and obtain for us the blessing we need both for this present life and for the life which has no end.

And that is what we do in this prayer, whatever the precise origins of the words themselves may be. Just as we instinctively turn to our earthly mothers for help when we make mistakes, we as sinners ask Mary, our heavenly mother, to intercede for us with God, our Father.

The Glory Be

> Glory be to the Father, the Son, and the Holy Spirit; as it was in the beginning, is now, and ever shall be, world without end. Amen.

A "doxology" is any short prayer of praise to God. The Glory Be, the doxology that Catholics are most familiar with, is used in the Rosary and gives praise to the triune God. We recall that from "the beginning," God's divine presence, or "glory," has permeated all of creation and will do so always and everywhere. The version of this prayer that many Catholics remember and continue to use ends with the phrase "world without end," whereas a more recent version found in some collections of prayers uses the phrase "now and forever." While the latter phrase probably says more clearly what the prayer means to say, the former is undeniably more poetic and carries more of the mystery to which the words refer.

Some, though certainly not all, who pray the Rosary add a short prayer called the Fátima Prayer because it originated in the context of a vision reported by one of the children believed to have seen the Blessed Virgin at Fátima, Portugal, in 1917 (more on this in Appendix B). This prayer, for those who choose to pray it, follows the Glory Be at the end of each of the Rosary's five decades:

> O my Jesus, forgive us our sins, save us from the fires of hell, and lead all souls to heaven, especially those in most need of thy (your) mercy. Amen.

The Hail Holy Queen or Salve Regina

> Hail, holy Queen, mother of mercy, our life, our sweetness, and our hope. To you we cry, poor banished children of Eve; to you we send up our sighs, mourning and weeping in this valley of tears. Turn, then, most gracious advocate, your eyes of mercy toward us; and after this, our exile, show unto us the blessed fruit of your womb, Jesus. O clement, O loving, O sweet Virgin Mary.

Customarily, the Rosary concludes with the recitation of the Salve Regina, the title of which means "Hail, Holy Queen." This classic prayer for Mary's intercession is striking for its imagery and for its poetic cadence. An updated version of the prayer uses modern pronouns and substitutes slightly different wording (some of which are indicated in parentheses).

"Hail, Holy Queen, mother of mercy, our life, our sweetness, and our hope." In this prayer, we first call upon Mary as "holy Queen" and "mother of mercy." Mary is Mother of Mercy in a double sense—both because she is merciful and because Jesus, her son, is the fullest expression possible of God's mercy. We can turn to Mary in times of need because she is "our life, our sweetness, and our hope."

"To thee (you) we cry, poor banished children of Eve; to thee (you) we send up our sighs, mourning and weeping in this vale (valley) of tears." The second sentence of the prayer states the central motive in calling upon Mary for help, namely, the experience of human anguish and sorrow. We refer to ourselves as pitiful "banished children of Eve." A later line in the original version (and the same line in the updated version) refers to our condition as "exile." As "children of Eve," we recognize that we are sinners.

To call ourselves "banished" may seem incongruous in the light of the Incarnation and redemption of Christ, for in him we are in fact no longer banished. (The updated version of the prayer actually deletes that phrase.) However, because we are still on a pilgrimage and because our salvation is incomplete on this side of eternity, the words of the prayer do describe a real dimension of our experience in this life. A constant underlying theme of our experience is one of incompleteness in this world, and that is what this part of the prayer expresses.

The prayer dates to Europe in the Middle Ages, when many people experienced lives of great physical hardship. The "valley of tears" was their earthly condition, from which heaven would release them "after this, our exile."

"Turn then, most gracious advocate, thine (your) eyes of mercy toward us . . ." The prayer acknowledges that Mary is our advocate with Jesus and asks for her mercy, her assistance in our earthly life.

". . . and after this, our exile, show unto us the blessed fruit of thy (your) womb, Jesus." Finally, the prayer asks Mary for the ultimate gift of union with Christ following death. The updated version is more active in tone, substituting "lead us home at last" for "after this, our exile."

"O clement, O loving, O sweet Virgin Mary." The prayer concludes with another expression of praise for Mary. The archaic adjective "clement" means "inclined to be lenient or merciful."

When the Rosary is prayed in a group, the leader may add, *"Pray for us, O Holy Mother of God,"* which the congregation concludes by responding, *"that we may be made worthy of the promises of Christ."*

The Hail, Holy Queen is often given beautiful musical expression in its Latin original, as a Gregorian chant. If you have never heard this chanted version of the prayer in Latin, be sure to locate and listen to a recording of it.

CHAPTER 4

MOMENTS FOR MEDITATION

The Twenty Mysteries of the Rosary

I love a good mystery—especially when the detective assembles all the clues and cleverly identifies the murderer, etc., etc. Clever detective that I fancied myself to be in my youth, however, I couldn't figure out what the word "mystery" had to do with the events that we meditate upon in the Rosary. The problem, I soon learned, wasn't in the Rosary but rather in my understanding of the meaning of "mystery." Upon consulting a dictionary, I learned that circumstances that require ingenuity for a solution are not properly called "mysteries" at all but rather puzzles, and that the term "mystery" is correctly defined as "a religious truth that one can know only by revelation and cannot fully understand."[12] Thus, the term "mystery" is often applied to events whereby God's self-revelation in human history took place.

Each of the mysteries of the Rosary is an event whereby God revealed both himself and his love for humankind, particularly in the context of his entrance into creation and human history in the person of Jesus of Nazareth. Each event has its unique characteristics, and each reveals something special about God's love, but each also reveals a reality that far transcends the grasp

of the human mind. In this sense, each is and remains a revelation of the mystery of God's love.

The mysteries as we know them today emerged in roughly
three stages. First, during the twelfth century, it became the custom among Christians, when praying, to recite a phrase refer-
ring to a significant event in the life of Jesus or Mary prior to
reciting one of the psalms. Eventually, the psalms were dropped,
and this way of praying consisted only of reflecting on the events
in the life of Jesus or Mary.

Second, during the thirteenth and fourteenth centuries, the
custom developed of focusing on various joyful events in the
life of Mary from the Gospels. Often the recitation of this "joy"
was accompanied by saying a Hail Mary. One might, for example, recite fifty joyful meditations from the life of Mary, joined
by fifty Hail Marys. During the fourteenth century, this devotion expanded to include the "sorrows" from the life of Mary
as well as her "joys" in heaven. Eventually, it became standard
practice to recite fifty earthly joys of Mary, fifty earthly sorrows,
and fifty heavenly joys (glorious mysteries), each one paired
with a Hail Mary.

The final stage in the development of the Rosary mysteries
took place in the fifteenth century. Up until this point, meditation on the events in Mary's life was useful only to those who
could read, because it was impossible to remember 150 meditations. Each meditation had to be written down, and that
excluded people who were illiterate—which, at the time, was
almost everybody. So that the meditations could be accessible
to everyone, the list was cut to fifteen, five for each set of meditations, and paired with 150 Hail Marys—ten Hail Marys per
"mystery." At this point, the meditations, or mysteries, became

focal points for recitation of the Hail Marys and, combined with repetitions of the Our Father and the Glory Be, became the Rosary more or less as we know it today. This way of organizing the Rosary first appeared in print in a book published in 1483 titled *Our Dear Lady's Psalter.*

A major change happened in 2002, when Pope St. John Paul II added five "luminous" mysteries to the fifteen joyful, sorrowful, and glorious mysteries. The pope also suggested the practice, which many people find helpful, of concluding each mystery "with *a prayer for the fruits specific to that particular mystery."* "In this way," the pontiff went on to say, "the Rosary would better express its connection with the Christian life" (*Rosarium Virginis Mariae,* 35).

Thus, the Rosary continues to be a living, active part of our faith. Although all the mysteries can be prayed any time you like, they are typically associated with certain days of the week or with particular liturgical seasons.

The Joyful Mysteries

Traditionally prayed on Mondays and Saturdays and on Sundays during Advent

Like all the mysteries of the Rosary, the joyful mysteries describe events that are central to what theologians call "the Christ event." The joyful mysteries relate to the Incarnation, that is, the becoming human and coming into history of Jesus the Christ. If anything is particularly mysterious about these events, it is how deeply ordinary and human each one is. Nothing is more common than the conception and birth of an infant, and yet nothing is more miraculous. If the joyful mysteries share something in common, it is the presence of the holy in the ordinary. On the surface, each one is as ordinary as the day is long: a young woman becomes pregnant; she visits her pregnant cousin; she gives birth to a baby; she and her husband take their infant son to fulfill the traditions of their religion. Yet each event is also utterly unique, carrying the presence of God into time and space in a once-and-for-all, unrepeatable way that changes everything forever.

1. The Annunciation: Authentic Faith Is Open to the Unexpected

Fruit of the Mystery: Humility

In the sixth month the angel Gabriel was sent by God to a town in Galilee called Nazareth, to a virgin engaged to a man whose name was Joseph, of the house of David. The virgin's name was Mary. And he came to her and said, "Greetings, favored one! The Lord is with you." But she was much perplexed by his words and pondered what sort of greeting this might be. The angel said to her, "Do not be afraid, Mary, for you have found favor with God. And now, you will conceive in your womb and bear a son, and you will name him Jesus. He will be great, and will be called the Son of the Most High, and the Lord God will give to him the throne of his ancestor David. He will reign over the house of Jacob forever, and of his kingdom there will be no end." Mary said to the angel,

"How can this be, since I am a virgin?" The angel said to her, "The Holy Spirit will come upon you, and the power of the Most High will overshadow you; therefore the child to be born will be holy; he will be called Son of God. And now, your relative Elizabeth in her old age has also conceived a son; and this is the sixth month for her who was said to be barren. For nothing will be impossible with God." Then Mary said, "Here am I, the servant of the Lord; let it be with me according to your word." Then the angel departed from her.

—Luke 1:26-38

The annunciation is one of the most dramatic events in all of the Gospels. We are so familiar with the narrative, however, that we tend to read it, or hear it read, in a rather blasé frame of mind. We know all about it, we think. We know the characters—Mary and the angel Gabriel. We already know who says what and when. And we know how the story ends. Ho hum. We've heard it so many times before!

We are well advised, however, to give ourselves a mental wake-up call so that we will read with our eyes really open and our minds truly alert. This narrative, like countless narratives throughout Scripture, is packed with astonishing details that we routinely miss. Also it is not without its humorous aspects.

Pay close attention to what happens here. The first character we are introduced to is "the angel Gabriel." The first hearers, and later the first readers, of this account were Jewish. They knew perfectly well from the Old Testament who the angel Gabriel was. Gabriel was the heavenly messenger who interpreted King Nebuchadnezzar's dream for Daniel (Daniel

8:15-27). In that narrative, Gabriel was God's instrument to reveal the superiority of the wisdom of Israel's God over the worldly wisdom of the pagans.

The fact that Gabriel is the angel who visits Mary suggests the superiority of the revelation Gabriel is about to speak to Mary. This fact is also a direct inference that the birth of Jesus will fulfill the prophecy spoken by Gabriel to Daniel in Daniel 9:20-26.

Luke introduces his narrative by stating simply that everything he is about to tell us took place in "a town in Galilee called Nazareth." This sentence sets the stage, and what it told Luke's first audience was that the following event happened in the most obscure and least important of places—in a word, Hicksville. Nazareth was Nowhere. Nothing important had ever happened there, and nobody important lived there or was even from there. It was the least likely place for the Son of God to be conceived. To say that Jesus had "humble" beginnings doesn't even come close!

Gabriel went to Nazareth, the story goes, to see "a virgin" whose "name was Mary." Apart from the fact that she was engaged to Joseph, that's all we are told about her. In his article "The Historical Mary," Fr. Robert P. Maloney, CM, provides insights into this obscure young woman. Given the name "Miriam," after the sister of Moses, Mary was a poor peasant girl of about thirteen or fourteen years old who spoke Aramaic with a Galilean accent. But she also may have had a passing familiarity with the Latin spoken by the soldiers of the Roman occupation; with Greek, which was the language of the marketplace; and, of course, with Hebrew, which was spoken in the synagogue.[13]

As familiar as we are with this story, the Gospel of Luke goes to some lengths to show us that the events that take place are anything but predictable. First, an angel appears to Mary (hardly an everyday occurrence) and greets her. Yet all Luke tells us is that Mary is "much perplexed" by Gabriel's words to her, when all he has said so far is "Greetings, favored one [recall: *kecharitōmenē* / *gratia plena* / full of grace]! The Lord is with you." Still, it's clear that Gabriel's words give young Mary pause. At first she says nothing in response to the angel and bides her time, pondering "what sort of greeting this might be."

So Gabriel speaks again, reassuring Mary, "Do not be afraid," and explaining why there is no need to be anxious or fearful. Nothing we have been told so far tells us that Mary was afraid, but apparently, that's how the angel interpreted her silence. The reason Mary shouldn't be afraid, Gabriel continues, is that she has "found favor with God," but once again, Mary remains silent.

Gabriel keeps right on delivering his message all the same, informing young Mary that "now" she "will conceive in [her] womb and bear a son." And if that isn't enough, Gabriel forges ahead—still no pause for a reaction—and informs Mary that she "will name him Jesus." And still no response from Mary!

Then comes the second part of Gabriel's verbal one-two punch. He instructs Mary, telling her that the infant she will give birth to "will be called the Son of the Most High, and the Lord God will give to him the throne of his ancestor David." These words are loaded. The Old Testament refers to God as "the Most High" a total of 109 times, so there is no question of who Gabriel is talking about here. He tells Mary, point-blank, that the baby she is going to conceive and give birth to is God's own Son.

By this time in the narrative, you would think that Mary would be at least stammering, "But . . . but . . . but. . . ." Not so, however; still, she says nothing. But if she was "pondering" on Gabriel's words when all he did was to greet her, by now she must have been doing some *major* pondering. Things just keep getting "curiouser and curiouser."

The angel finishes dropping his verbal bomb with remarks about how God will give the son Mary will bear "the throne of his ancestor David," how this son will "reign over the house of Jacob forever," and how his "kingdom" will have "no end." Luke doesn't tell us whether Mary was standing or sitting when Gabriel arrived, but if she was standing in the beginning, you'd think that she would definitely be sitting down by now.

Regardless, Mary finally speaks. Given all the talking Gabriel has done, it's almost as if this is the first time Mary can get a word in edgewise, and her question is a perfectly sensible one. She bypasses all the talk of thrones and kingdoms and gets right down to practicalities. Mary knows a thing or two about where babies come from, and so she asks, "How can this be, since I am a virgin?"

This question makes sense, but remember the situation. An *angel*, for crying out loud, shows up and lays a rather long, impressive message on young Mary, but it's as if she's not all that impressed! She doesn't let loose with the first-century Palestinian equivalent of "No way!" or "Yeah, right!" She doesn't ask, "Who the heck are you, anyway?" No, she seems to take the angel at his word. But she also has her question. Even from an angel, she wants an answer, thank you very much—no disrespect intended.

For his part, Gabriel doesn't stand on formalities. He doesn't fall back on his credentials and say, "Hey, I'm an angel—I know what I'm talking about, okay? Don't you worry your little head about how this is going to happen. Just keep quiet and do as you're told." No, Mary asks a sensible, understandable question, and Gabriel is happy to give a straightforward reply: "The Holy Spirit will come upon you, and the power of the Most High will overshadow you; therefore the child to be born will be holy; he will be called Son of God."

Again, Mary remains silent! Scripture scholars tell us that it's indisputable that the theological point Luke wants to make here is that Mary became pregnant as a virgin. Theologically, Luke means this to say more about Jesus than about Mary. The main reason for making this point isn't to glorify virginity or denigrate sex, especially sexual intimacy in marriage. The main reason for emphasizing that Jesus had no biological human father is to make it clear that he is the Son of God.

At the same time, this point makes clear the completely human nature of Jesus' entrance into space and time. He gets his humanity from a fully human mother. He is, in other words, fully divine and fully human, and neither fact may be downplayed at the expense of the other.

But Gabriel isn't done yet. Here comes bombshell number two. Mary's elderly cousin Elizabeth, whom everyone thought was unable to have a baby, is already six months pregnant. "For nothing," Gabriel explains, "will be impossible with God"—the implication being that if God can do this for Elizabeth, then he can darn well do what Gabriel has just told Mary is going to happen to her.

Mary's final response to the angel is to express complete openness to God's will for her life: "Here am I, the servant of the Lord; let it be with me according to your word." She might as well have said, "If God wants me to be of service to him in some way, I'm fine with that, no matter what it is." Luke concludes his narrative by telling us that the angel took his leave.

Reflecting on this narrative—this first joyful mystery—in the context of the Rosary, we can learn much about the nature of Christian faith, and it all comes down to a single idea: ultimately, faith means openness to God's will and trusting acceptance of his call, no matter what demands it makes upon us, no matter what risks it brings with it.

We can look at it this way. We will never experience anything even remotely as dramatic as what happened to Mary, it's true. But all the same, angels bearing God's will for us come into our lives each and every day, if only we are prepared to recognize them. They speak to us in the everyday events of our ordinary lives. They whisper to us words like "Be patient with that child" or "that teenager" or "your spouse" or "your fellow employee." Angels also whisper words such as "Love your young adult offspring by telling him that it's time to get a job and move out."

Angels beckon us in all kinds of ordinary ways every day to act on God's will, so that we, too, may become instruments of God's loving presence in our little corner of the world. Young Mary also sets an example of what authentic adult faith looks like. She listens closely to the angel, but she also shows no signs of "blind faith." She does show signs of doubt, however. She doubts that it's possible for her to conceive a child except by the usual method. Therefore, she asks her question. This is because faith and doubt are by no means mutually exclusive. Having doubts and asking questions go hand in hand with adult faith.

The angel's response to Mary's question does nothing to clear things up, however—especially as far as a modern, scientific mind-set is concerned but even for Mary, in her time and place. The angel's reply is simply that God will take care of it, which is good enough for Mary. From this we can learn that even when we don't get clear, scientific answers to our questions, and when we still have our doubts, we can trust in God's wisdom and love. The bottom line is that we need to believe, with Mary as our model of faith, that "nothing will be impossible with God."

No matter what happens to us and no matter what happens in our lives, we can always make Mary's final words to the angel our words too: "Here am I, the servant of the Lord; let it be with me according to your word."

Let us not, however, miss the importance of Luke's final sentence in his annunciation narrative, namely, "Then the angel departed from her" (1:38). It would be easy as can be to disregard these words; in fact, that's what we usually and automatically do. But as best-selling author Fr. James Martin, SJ, points out, "This is the part about faith. This is where we live."

In other words, we live in the era that began after the angel "departed" and left Mary with the consequences of her choice. Now as never before, faith—an ongoing commitment to, loving intimacy with, and complete trust in the triune God—is "where it's at" for us.

2. The Visitation: Authentic Faith Inspires Us to Make Sacrifices for Others

Fruit of the Mystery: Love of Neighbor

> In those days Mary set out and went with haste to a Judean town in the hill country, where she entered the house of Zechariah and greeted Elizabeth. When Elizabeth heard Mary's greeting, the child leaped in her womb. And Elizabeth was filled with the Holy Spirit and exclaimed with a loud cry, "Blessed are you among women, and blessed is the fruit of your womb. . . ."
>
> And Mary remained with [Elizabeth] about three months and then returned to her home.
>
> —Luke 1:39-42, 56

The next thing we know, Mary hotfoots it to the home of her elderly relative Elizabeth. Luke is vague—"in those days," he writes—about how soon after Gabriel's visit Mary hits the road, but we may presume that it was only a matter of days.

Our curiosity may run a little wild at this point. Did Mary tell her parents what had happened to her? Did she wonder how she would explain this to the neighbors or her friends? Did Mary get an anxiety attack after the angel left and start wondering what she was going to do now? It would seem only natural, even if she was now involved with the supernatural up to her eyeballs.

We're left with our curiosity, however, since Luke speaks only about what God did and is doing. Perhaps that was all that Luke thought his audience needed or wanted to know.

Apparently, if "in those days" Mary did any spiritual or emotional wrestling with herself—and it would be perfectly human if she did—before long she sets aside any preoccupation with herself and thinks of Elizabeth, who no doubt could use the company and help of her younger relative. Luke tells us nothing about the journey itself, only that when Mary arrives, the infant John (the Baptist) in Elizabeth does a little in utero flip. Then Elizabeth gives voice to what will become the next part of the Hail Mary, after the angel's greeting: "Blessed are you among women, and blessed is the fruit of your womb."

So not only does Mary know about Elizabeth's remarkable pregnancy, but somehow Elizabeth has also learned about Mary's miraculous pregnancy. The Gospel of Luke's theological purpose, of course, is to relate the two blessed events and to link Jesus and John the Baptist, even before they are born. Elizabeth speaks for the entire Christian community down through history when she adds, "And blessed is she [Mary] who believed that there would be a fulfillment of what was spoken to her by the Lord" (1:45).

Following Mary's Magnificat ("My soul magnifies the Lord"), which runs from verses 46 to 55—one of the greatest and most beautiful canticles, or songs, in the entire Bible, but not immediately relevant to our focus here—Luke concludes by informing us that Mary's visit with Elizabeth lasted "about three months." Since we learned from Gabriel that Elizabeth was already six months into her pregnancy, we may conclude that Mary remained with Elizabeth either until just prior to John's birth or until just after John was born. The following verses say nothing about Mary being present for the birth, however, so again we are left guessing. Theologically, it would be interesting if Mary were present to assist with the delivery of John the Baptist, but any suggestion that this was the case must remain pure speculation.

As we pray the Rosary, this mystery is a terrific reminder of the humanity of Mary and of the importance to her of extended family relationships. Even when she has had the most amazing experience herself, she thinks not of herself but of the needs of her elderly cousin. Clearly the central focus in young Mary's life is already the message that her son will proclaim—that the purpose of life is love of God and neighbor.

3. The Nativity: Authentic Faith Discovers the Glorious in the Ordinary

Fruit of the Mystery: Poverty

In those days a decree went out from Emperor Augustus that all the world should be registered. This was the first registration and was taken while Quirinius was governor of Syria. All went to their own towns to be registered. Joseph also went from the town of Nazareth in Galilee to Judea, to the city of David called Bethlehem, because he was descended from the house and family of David. He went to be registered with Mary, to whom he was engaged and who was expecting a child. While they were

> there, the time came for her to deliver her child. And she gave birth to her firstborn son and wrapped him in bands of cloth, and laid him in a manger, because there was no place for them in the inn.
>
> —Luke 2:1-7

The infancy narrative in the Gospel of Luke—from which this short selection comes—is familiar to anyone who has ever attended church services on Christmas, even if that's the only day in the year he or she went anywhere near a church. For that matter, it's familiar to anyone who ever saw the late cartoonist Charles Schulz's animated television feature *A Charlie Brown Christmas*. It's common, however, for people to take this narrative as nothing more than charming Christmas nostalgia, missing the meanings intended by the Gospel that were easily understood by those who first heard it.

Luke makes sure to situate his account of the birth of Jesus historically. That's why he informs us that it was a very particular Roman emperor, Augustus, who demanded that a census be taken for the first time. Not only that, but it was the governor named Quirinius who was in office, not some other governor at some other time. This is Luke's way of saying, "I didn't make this up; it really happened, and this is when and where it happened."

Next, we get a genealogical note. Luke writes that Joseph took Mary to Bethlehem to register for the census because that was the hometown for everyone in the family line, which traced its origins back to the prominent Jewish king, David.

Thus, even though Jesus' Father is the God of Israel, through his human foster father too, Jesus comes from a royal lineage.

From Luke's observation that the newborn Messiah ended up in a feed box for animals, we may conclude that the birth took place in a shack or cave, a shelter for cattle, or something along those lines. The couple was unable to find a room at any of Bethlehem's first-century equivalents of a motel—which makes sense given the huge influx of people into Bethlehem for the census.

Miriam, "Mary" to us, gives birth to a baby boy and wraps him in "swaddling clothes" or "bands of cloth"—depending on the translation you're reading—and places him in "a manger," i.e., a feed box for animals. Luke doesn't mention it, but we may assume that before wrapping the baby up and putting him to bed, the new mother would first have cuddled and breastfed him, all the while gazing at him with wonder and praising God for the miracle of her baby.

The theological purpose at hand is, first, to declare that Jesus' birth was an actual historical event and, second, to illustrate the poverty and anonymity of his birth. The Son of the King of the universe arrives in the usual, thoroughly ordinary human manner. Jesus doesn't fly in on a cloud with angels blowing trumpets in order to stun the whole world with his power and majesty. Obscure, poor, and gloriously ordinary—that's how the Messiah and Son of God arrives.

Reflecting on this mystery in the context of the Rosary, we may want to rethink any romantic notions we may have about the meaning of Christmas. For the true joy of Christmas has nothing to do with most of what goes on in the name of the annual "holiday shopping season." Indeed, the contemporary tendency in the marketplace to replace the greeting "Merry Christmas" with "Happy Holidays" should encourage us to treasure even more the Church-related situations where we may use the former greeting as a true expression of faith.

4. The Presentation: Authentic Faith Is Open to the Prophetic Word

Fruit of the Mystery: Obedience

> When the time came for their purification according to the law of Moses, they brought him up to Jerusalem to present him to the Lord.
>
> —Luke 2:22

According to Jewish custom, Mary was required to present herself in the Temple to be "purified" following Jesus' birth, because under Jewish law, she was ritually impure after giving birth. Bible scholars remain puzzled by the reference here to "their" purification. The way the original Greek is constructed, it must refer to both Mary and Joseph, but this makes no sense because Jewish law made no provision for the purification of the husband, only that of the wife.

In addition to Mary's purification, the law required that a firstborn son be consecrated to the Lord with a sacrifice. Underscoring the poverty of Mary and Joseph, Luke's Gospel tells us that they brought one of the sacrifices that was offered by poor couples, namely, "a pair of turtledoves or two young pigeons" (2:24).

When they arrive at the Temple, the little family encounters old Simeon, whom Luke describes as "righteous and devout, looking forward to the consolation of Israel, and the Holy Spirit rested on him" (2:25). Not only that, but Luke says, "It had been revealed to him by the Holy Spirit that he would not see death before he had seen the Lord's Messiah" (2:26). All this, as well as everything that follows, restates for us that the birth of Jesus was a major manifestation of the holy in an ordinary, everyday event.

Simeon goes on at some length about the impact Jesus will have and the consequences for Mary herself. Then along comes the devout elderly Anna, who adds her prophetic comments to those of Simeon. Luke comments that Anna began to "speak about the child to all who were looking for the redemption of Jerusalem" (2:38). One may wonder whether this kind of talk in Jerusalem, where people from all around came to the Temple, may have spread to Mary and Joseph's close-knit hometown of Nazareth. One might think that the gossip mill would have shifted into overdrive.

According to Luke, Mary and Joseph were startled by the words of Simeon and Anna. They "were amazed," Luke says (2:33). Given everything that Luke already told us about events prior to and at the time of Jesus' birth, we may justifiably be puzzled by Mary's and Joseph's amazement in the Temple. What with the angel Gabriel announcing Jesus' conception, and angels and shepherds showing up when Jesus was born, and the magi coming around, one would think that by now Mary and Joseph would be less likely to be amazed by anything where Jesus was concerned. But not so.

Of course, we do well to keep in mind that the main concern of the Gospel of Luke is to make theological rather than historical points, and so the reason for the Gospel's remarks about Mary's and Joseph's continued amazement may have more to do with Luke's ongoing intention to point out who Jesus is than to provide us with a literal description of how Mary and Joseph reacted to what Simeon and Anna said. At the same time, if the human author of Luke's Gospel got his information from Mary herself—which may or may not be the case— years after the events described by the Gospel, years after the death and resurrection of Jesus, the amazement might understandably be recalled as greater than it actually was.

No matter what the facts may be, however, the overall meaning of the presentation of the infant Jesus in the Temple is clear from the words of Simeon, which all believers can make their own: "My eyes have seen your salvation, / which you have prepared in the presence of all peoples, / a light for revelation to the Gentiles and for glory to your people Israel" (Luke 2:30-32).

As a mystery of the Rosary, the presentation is an inspiration to cherish our own relationship with Mary as her children in Christ. Just as she and Joseph presented the infant Christ in the Temple, so Mary constantly presents us to Jesus with her love for us all.

5. The Finding of Jesus in the Temple: Authentic Faith Doesn't Cling to Preconceived Notions

Fruit of the Mystery: Joy in Finding Jesus

Now every year his parents went to Jerusalem for the festival of the Passover. And when he was twelve years old, they went up as usual for the festival. When the festival was ended and they started to return, the boy Jesus stayed behind in Jerusalem, but his parents did not know it. Assuming that he was in the group of travelers, they went a day's journey. Then they started to look for him among their relatives and friends. When they did not find him, they returned to Jerusalem to search for him. After three days they found him in the temple, sitting among the teachers, listening to them and asking them questions. And all who heard him were amazed at his understanding and his answers. When his parents saw him they were astonished; and his mother said to him, "Child, why have you treated us like this? Look, your father and I have been searching for you in great anxiety." He said to them, "Why were you searching for me? Did you not know that I must be in my Father's house?" But they did not understand what he said to them. Then he went down with them and came to Nazareth, and was obedient to them. His mother treasured all these things in her heart.

And Jesus increased in wisdom and in years, and in divine and human favor.

—Luke 2:41-52

The last of the five joyful mysteries comes from a familiar event found only in the Gospel of Luke. Again, many commentators on Luke, down through the centuries, see this as evidence that the author of Luke may have had direct testimony from Mary herself. Whether or not this is the case, Luke's account of the loss and finding of the boy Jesus in the Temple in Jerusalem is filled with a wealth of insights.

First, we learn from Luke that it was a yearly custom for Mary, Joseph, and Jesus to journey to Jerusalem for the Passover festival. Then, he tells us that at this particular time, Jesus was twelve years old. Keep in mind that twelve was considered a more mature age in that time and culture than it is in our own. Twelve was on the verge of adulthood. Indeed, it's no accident that even today it is at the age of twelve that Jewish boys and girls celebrate Judaism's coming-of-age rituals, bar mitzvah (for boys) and bat mitzvah (for girls).

Luke tells us nothing about what Mary, Joseph, and Jesus did at the festival itself, only that when it was time to make the return trek to Nazareth, Mary and Joseph took it for granted that Jesus was "in the group of travelers." Based on past experience, apparently, they had no reason to think otherwise for an entire day. It was that long before it dawned on Mary and Joseph that Jesus wasn't in the "group of travelers" at all.

So there they are, a day's travel from Jerusalem, and they discover that they must turn around and go back. That's two days that Jesus is missing by the time they get back to Jerusalem. Think about it. How would any parent feel if a child was missing for two days? Then when they arrive back in Jerusalem, Luke tells us, they look for Jesus for three more days before they find him. So that's five days all together that Jesus was missing. Put yourself in their place. How would any parent feel if a child were missing for five days? Are we talking frantic here or what?

Finally, Mary and Joseph discover the twelve-year-old Jesus in, of all places, the Temple. Notice that no way was the Temple the first place they looked for Jesus. They searched high and low for three days before they even thought to look in the Temple. So much for pious notions of the boy Jesus. Apparently, Mary and Joseph did not think of him as the kind of boy who was likely to be hanging out in the Temple. First they looked in the marketplaces, in the homes, perhaps, of friends and relatives, maybe in whatever were the ancient equivalents of today's "hang out" spots for youngsters.

Anyway, after five days, Mary and Joseph find their wayward sheep "sitting among the teachers, listening to them and asking them questions." Luke reports that Jesus was basically knocking everyone's socks off with "his understanding and his answers." A gifted child!

Luke says that Jesus' "parents . . . were astonished." A dictionary defines "astonished" as "being filled with sudden wonder or amazement." Note that being astonished is not incompatible with being "fit to be tied," which would only be natural for Mary and Joseph at this moment. In fact, the first words out of Mary's mouth express just such feelings.

"Child, why have you treated us like this?" Mary asks, with admirable restraint, we might say. In other words, Mary asks her twelve-year-old son how he could have been so thoughtless and insensitive. Didn't he care that she and Joseph had been worried sick? For *five days*. Why didn't he at the very least get a message to them through someone else in their traveling group so that they would have known where he was and what he was up to?

It would be perfectly understandable if Mary and Joseph had said at this moment, "You get yourself out of this Temple right now, young man! Now we have to walk all the way back to Nazareth by ourselves. You're grounded for a month, and at that you should consider yourself fortunate! Don't you ever pull a stunt like this again, do you hear me?" Or words to this effect.

Luke doesn't report that Mary and Joseph said anything like this, of course. Instead, Mary tells Jesus what should have been obvious to him, that they had been looking everywhere "in great anxiety." Instead of apologizing, however, Jesus replies, apparently calmly, that Mary and Joseph should have known that he had to be in his "Father's house," or as other translations would have it, "about [his] Father's interests."

Whatever Mary and Joseph thought about Jesus' response— perhaps that he was being thoughtless and insensitive—Luke remarks that they had no idea what their son was talking about. In other words, they were clueless. Mary and Joseph may have said something like, "Come on, we're going home now," but whether they did or not, Jesus evidently knew that his little adventure was over.

Luke's concluding words about this event tell us that young Jesus went back to Nazareth with Mary and Joseph and (from then on, anyway) "was obedient to them." Lesson learned. Apparently, even if at that particular moment in the Temple Jesus resembled a smart-mouthed kid, he seems to have learned from his mistake. What a deeply insightful and human observation Luke makes—and how easy it is to believe that his words come from conversations he may have had with Mary herself in later years—when he remarks that she "treasured all these things in her heart." What mother wouldn't?

Luke's final words, telling us all we know about Jesus' so-called hidden years, are filled with both poetry and theological insight: "And Jesus increased in wisdom and in years, and in divine and human favor" (2:52).

The Sorrowful Mysteries

Traditionally prayed on Tuesdays and Fridays and on Sundays during Lent

This group of mysteries of the Rosary all come from the passion narratives in the Gospels, that is, the Gospels' accounts of the torture and execution of Jesus by crucifixion. Once again, they are all concerned with a key event in the redemption and salvation of the world, and once again, each one looks, on the surface, as ordinary as can be. A man agonizes over his impending torture and death. He is tortured and mocked by his executioners. His executioners force him to drag the cross upon which he will be crucified to the place where his execution will take place. Finally, nails, driven through his feet and wrists, pin him to the cross, and he dies a long and agonizing death. Especially for the era in which it occurred, it all looked so ordinary. But who the man was who suffered and died—that's what makes all the difference.

Each mystery carries an infinitely holy meaning and purpose that change everything for all time. By his incarnation, suffering, death, and resurrection, Jesus accomplishes the redemption of the world. These mysteries tell us of the suffering and death phase, if you will, of the event that brought about our salvation.

1. The Agony in the Garden: Authentic Faith Abandons Self to God, No Matter What

Fruit of the Mystery: Sorrow for Sin

> They went to a place called Gethsemane; and he said to his disciples, "Sit here while I pray." He took with him Peter and James and John, and began to be distressed and agitated. And he said to them, "I am deeply grieved, even to death; remain here, and keep awake." And going a little farther, he threw himself on the ground and prayed that, if it were possible, the hour might pass from him. He said, "Abba, Father, for you all things are possible; remove this cup from me; yet, not what I want, but what you want."
>
> —Mark 14:32-36

The Gospels of Matthew, Mark, and Luke all describe Jesus' agony in the Garden of Gethsemane. The Gospel of John—unique in many ways—mentions only that Jesus "went out with his disciples across the Kidron valley to a place where there was a garden, which he and his disciples entered" (18:1).

The Gospel of Mark, quoted here, is the oldest and linguistically the most primitive of the four Gospels. It uses strong, graphic language to describe Jesus' experience in the garden. Mark says that Jesus was "distressed and agitated." The older Revised Standard Version translates these words as "greatly distressed and troubled." The point, however, is that Mark has no doubt about how human Jesus' anguish was as he anticipated the hours ahead of him.

The Gospel of Matthew, not as old as Mark's Gospel and probably a little older than the Gospel of Luke, says that in the Garden of Gethsemane, Jesus "began to be grieved and agitated." Then Jesus speaks for himself, saying, "I am deeply grieved, even to death" (Matthew 26:37, 38).

Luke's passion narrative parallels those of Mark and Matthew and also includes elements that are both divine and uniquely human:

> Then he withdrew from them about a stone's throw, knelt down, and prayed, "Father, if you are willing, remove this cup from me; yet, not my will but yours be done." Then an angel from heaven appeared to him and gave him strength. In his anguish he prayed more earnestly, and his sweat became like great drops of blood falling down on the ground. (Luke 22:41-44)

For his own theological reasons, Luke remarks that Jesus was strengthened by an angel—perhaps to make more apparent to his readers the divine presence at this terrible hour. Then Luke describes Jesus' suffering in a unique and particularly graphic way, saying that Jesus' "sweat became like great drops of blood." There is no question that, in the opinion of these three Gospel writers, Jesus' experience in the garden was one of intense, painful anguish.

For those who pray the sorrowful mysteries of the Rosary, the model provided by Jesus here illustrates the need, in the midst of anxiety, stress, and fear, to abandon oneself to God, our loving Father. We do well in such circumstances to tell him clearly what we want, as Jesus did, and then abandon ourselves to his care, making the words of Jesus our own: "Not what I want, but what you want."

2. The Scourging at the Pillar: Authentic Faith Embraces Jesus' Humanity and Divinity

Fruit of the Mystery: Purity

> Then Pilate took Jesus and had him flogged.
> —John 19:1

All four Gospels say that Jesus was scourged, or flogged, but none mention a pillar. Perhaps we can attribute the inclusion of a pillar in the name of this mystery to the influence of artistic depictions down through the centuries that show Jesus tied to a pillar while being flogged. Or perhaps there was an assumption that a person being flogged would have had to be tied to something in order to be kept standing.

This second sorrowful mystery can't really be separated from the event that follows it in all four Gospels, namely, the third sorrowful mystery, the crowning with thorns. Down through the centuries, however, the second mystery has helped those who pray the Rosary to focus on the very real physical nature of Jesus' suffering at the hands of those who tortured him. It is particularly noteworthy that the scourging of Jesus appears in the fourth Gospel. This is one of the ways in which John emphasizes Jesus' humanity. It is remarkable in that John inclines heavily toward presenting Jesus in the light of his divinity, in ways that the other three Gospels do not.

For example, instead of giving us a fourth infancy narrative, John's Gospel begins with a unique prologue that calls Jesus "the Word" who "was with God, and . . . was God" (1:1). Yet the Gospel of John never goes so far as to ignore or even downplay Jesus' humanity. This mention of Jesus' flogging is but one example of how the fourth Gospel regularly shines a light on how fully human Jesus was, even as it places a unique emphasis on his divinity.

3. The Crowning with Thorns: Authentic Faith Shares in the Physical and Mental Suffering of Christ

Fruit of the Mystery: Courage

> And they clothed him in a purple cloak; and after twisting some thorns into a crown, they put it on him. And they began saluting him, "Hail, King of the Jews!" They struck his head with a reed, spat upon him, and knelt down in homage to him. After mocking him, they stripped him of the purple cloak and put his own clothes on him. Then they led him out to crucify him.
>
> —Mark 15:17-20

This event, which all four Gospels include, is both a detailed description of how Jesus was tortured before being crucified and an ironic presentation of Jesus' deepest identity and meaning. For in terms of his ultimate identity, he is King of the universe.

As one of the mysteries of the Rosary, however, this event in the passion of Jesus continues the Rosary's reminder to us of the extent to which Jesus went in order to fully embrace the experience of being human. If every human life includes anguish and suffering, darkness and pain; if being human means being misunderstood and rejected; if it means being on the receiving end of injustice, then Jesus felt what we all feel—only to a far greater extent than most of us will ever feel it.

Jesus didn't just come into the world, into time and space, and live a more or less ordinary human life. No. He knew great joy, to be sure, but his life included the deepest darkness and pain that any human life could ever know. This is how deep his love for us is—so deep that he accepted the worst that could happen. The crown of thorns that humans, in their ignorance and cruelty, pushed down onto his head and into his scalp tortured him with an intense physical pain, no doubt. But how often do we reflect on the psychic pain that Jesus must have also felt? It's only human to want to be accepted, appreciated, and loved by others. So along with his physical suffering, Jesus experienced the most intense psychic and spiritual pain as well.

As we ponder Jesus' crowning with thorns, we might well reflect on this psychic pain that he undoubtedly knew but that so rarely receives any attention. The crown of thorns might be understood, in fact, as a symbol for the psychic suffering of Jesus. Reflecting on this, then, we may come to a deeper appreciation of ways that our own psychic pain and mental anguish can, through our intimacy with Christ, be as much a sharing in his suffering as any physical suffering we may have to endure. And because our psychic suffering can be a sharing in the psychic pain of Jesus, it can be a sharing in his redemptive suffering too.

4. The Carrying of the Cross: Authentic Faith Moves Us Forward, Even during Trials and Tribulations

Fruit of the Mystery: Patience

> So they took Jesus; and carrying the cross by himself, he went out to what is called The Place of the Skull, which in Hebrew is called Golgotha.
>
> —John 19:16b-17

Of the four Gospels, only John—for its own theological purposes—says that Jesus carried his cross himself. Matthew, Mark, and Luke all say that after Jesus stumbled, Simon of Cyrene carried Jesus' cross for him to Golgotha—and not altogether willingly either. Carrying his cross himself or trudging along with Simon of Cyrene, the point is that Jesus' suffering continued—there was no letup. Carrying his cross or stumbling along with Simon of Cyrene, Jesus continued his pilgrimage to crucifixion and death, and all the way he had nothing to go on but faith.

Sometimes we forget that Jesus' divinity did not override his humanity. As he went to his execution, he had no "inside information," no special reassurance that his life and death would mean anything. He had to rely on faith, which meant for him—just as it does for us—trusting his Father in heaven. As he walked his path of horrible suffering to Golgotha, Jesus had to trust in his Father's loving care. He had to abandon himself to his unavoidable fate and trust that God's love was trustworthy. And that's exactly what we must do as well.

One lesson we might learn from this mystery of the Rosary is that when we encounter suffering—whatever form it takes—our best option is to unite ourselves to Christ as he keeps moving, trusting in the love of his Father. As we keep moving, we can make the human faith of Jesus our faith too. As we pray this mystery of the Rosary, we can give ourselves up to God's love, no matter the sorrows or pain life includes at the moment. And in doing this, we carry our cross united to Christ.

5. The Crucifixion: Authentic Faith Is a Sharing in the Death of Jesus

Fruit of the Mystery: Perseverance

> Then they brought Jesus to the place called Golgotha (which means the place of a skull). And they offered him wine mixed with myrrh; but he did not take it. And they crucified him, and divided his clothes among them, casting lots to decide what each should take. It was nine o'clock in the morning when they crucified him.
> —Mark 15:22-25

All four Gospels tell us of Jesus' crucifixion, and—consistent with the unique theological perspective of each Gospel—we can learn something special from each one. Mark's, which as we have already noted, is probably the oldest Gospel, keeps the details to a minimum and is the only one to state matter-of-factly the exact time of day when Jesus was crucified.

There may be something particularly sad, in fact, about the simple statement "It was nine o'clock in the morning when they crucified him." Here it is a new day, and it begins with the barbaric act—resulting from human brutality, ignorance, and fear—of nailing the Son of God to a cross. Mark's account of Jesus' crucifixion is simple and straightforward, and each sentence is worthy of our attention.

Mark sets the scene by explaining to his Gentile Christian audience that "Golgotha" means "the place of a skull." The skull is a symbol of death, even in our own culture. How appropriate the setting, Mark might have added, for here is the place where the most significant death in all of human history would occur.

We learn that before the soldiers crucified Jesus, they tried to make him drink a mixture of wine and myrrh, the latter being a mild painkiller. Could the soldiers have been motivated by some passing shadow of compassion? Regardless, Mark tells us that Jesus refused to drink. Did Jesus refuse the drugged wine because his love for humankind is so deep that he wanted to accept the fullness of human suffering and death without having it dulled even slightly?

With almost brutal simplicity, Mark tells us that "they crucified him." There was no need to explain what that meant, since it would have been obvious to Mark's first audience. Everyone knew about crucifixion: the nails through the wrists (New Testament Greek has no word for "wrist," and authorities on human physiology agree that only nails through the bones of the wrist could bear the full weight of the human body on a cross); the nails through the feet; and the hanging for hours until death occurred, not from loss of blood, but by sheer vivid pain and slow suffocation as the lungs collapsed under the weight of the body.

Finally, Mark includes the observation that, crass to the end, the soldiers cast "lots"—shot craps, in fact—to see who would keep Jesus' "clothes." This is how total Jesus' poverty was. He went to his death without even clothes on his back. Scholars agree that Jesus was undoubtedly crucified naked; the addition of a loincloth to the corpus on crucifixes is the result of a concern for modesty in later centuries.

Jesus dies in the depths of the most horrible and degrading human suffering and the most complete human poverty. And he does so without complaint, out of love for his Father and obedience to his Father's will and, ultimately, out of love for all humanity. The Gospel of John says it best: "No one has greater love than this, to lay down one's life for one's friends" (15:13).

The Glorious Mysteries

Traditionally prayed on Wednesdays and Sundays, although Sundays during Lent are traditionally sorrowful mystery days, and Sundays during Advent are joyful mystery days.

The first three glorious mysteries all come from the post-crucifixion narratives in the Gospels and the Acts of the Apostles. The fourth and fifth glorious mysteries are unique in that they come not from New Testament accounts but from sacred Tradition. As such, they illustrate the intimate, interdependent connection between Scripture and Tradition existing since the earliest days of Christianity. This connection Roman Catholicism honors and preserves now as it has for more than two thousand years.

The fourth and fifth glorious mysteries, the assumption and coronation of Mary, come from sacred Tradition, the same Tradition from which the Christian Scriptures came. Devotion to Mary is part of Christian tradition from its earliest days following the resurrection of Jesus. Indeed, there can be no doubt that Mary had a special place of honor among the apostles of Jesus for as long as she remained on this earth. It is impossible to believe otherwise. That is how far back our devotion to Mary goes.

So it is incidental that Scripture doesn't mention the two mysteries about Mary, her assumption and coronation. They are perfect reminders of the continuing importance and value of Tradition and illustrations of the theological balance that characterizes the Rosary. The Rosary is heavily scriptural, but these two mysteries call to our attention the constant blessings that sacred Tradition makes possible in the life of Christian faith. They also remind us of the unbreakable union that exists between Scripture and Tradition.

1. The Resurrection: Authentic Faith Experiences the Risen Christ

Fruit of the Mystery: Faith

When the sabbath was over, Mary Magdalene, and Mary the mother of James, and Salome bought spices, so that they might go and anoint him. And very early on the first day of the week, when the sun had risen, they went to the tomb. They had been saying to one another, "Who will roll away the stone for us from the entrance to the tomb?" When they looked up, they saw that the stone, which was very large, had already been rolled back. As they entered the tomb, they saw a young man, dressed in a white robe, sitting on the right side; and they were alarmed. But he said to them, "Do not be alarmed; you are looking for Jesus of Nazareth, who was crucified. He has been raised; he is not here. Look, there is the place they laid him. But go, tell his disciples and Peter that he is going ahead of you to Galilee; there you will see him, just as he told you."

—Mark 16:1-7

The resurrection of Christ is the event upon which the entire Christian faith depends. If the resurrection didn't happen, all Christian history and the faith of countless Christians for more than two thousand years would fall like a house of cards. In the familiar words of St. Paul, "If Christ has not been raised, your faith is futile" (1 Corinthians 15:17). To accept this assertion is one thing, however, and to even begin to understand it is quite another.

The first glorious mystery leads us to the resurrection narratives of all four Gospels, and each has its own audience in mind and its own theological perspective. It is worth your while to read slowly through each one, taking note of the similarities and differences. For our purposes, however, the words of the angel to "Mary Magdalene and the other Mary" (Matthew 28:1) are enough to start our reflections: "Do not be afraid; I know that you are looking for Jesus who was crucified. He is not here; for he has been raised" (Matthew 28:5-6).

Scripture scholars and theologians discuss and debate the meaning of "resurrection" *ad infinitum,* and better minds than ours have been boggled by it. There are those who tend to turn the resurrection into a holy magic show, while at the other extreme, there are those who would deny that anything unique at all happened to Jesus after he died. In the end, we must turn to the Gospel narratives, to the Church's ongoing experience of the risen Lord in its midst for more than two millennia, and, finally, to common sense.

We don't know what a hypothetical eyewitness to the resurrection of Jesus would have seen, and we never will. If anything is a mystery, it is the resurrection. And yet, if anything is available for us to experience in all kinds of ordinary and unpredictable ways, it is the risen Christ.

Sometimes I think that when it comes to the resurrection, we do better to listen to poets than to theologians. Native American poet Sherman Alexie's poem "Drum as Love, Fear, Prayer," in his book *The Summer of Black Widows*, includes a description of the meaning of the resurrection in words that are not pious but still breathe new life into our understanding of the resurrection:

> Then she tells me that Jesus is still here
> because Jesus was once here,
> and parts of Jesus are still floating in the air.
> She tells me Jesus' DNA is part of the collective DNA.
> She tells me we are all part
> of Jesus, we are all Jesus in part. She tells me to breathe deep
> during all of our storms
> because you can sometimes taste Jesus in a good, hard rain.[14]

The knack we need to develop is that of clinging simultaneously to both the mystery and the electricity—metaphorically speaking, of course—of the resurrection. Our best bet is to open ourselves to the mystery of the resurrection, open ourselves prayerfully to its power, and cling to it with all our might. Let the theologians ponder and debate. Their work is important, but in the everyday world, we need to "taste Jesus in a good, hard rain"—as well as in our neighbors and in all things ordinary and everyday. The resurrection isn't a nut to be cracked; it's an experience to be had. It isn't a problem to solve; it's a reality to love and embrace.

When we pray the first glorious mystery, we quietly celebrate not only the mystery at the heart of our faith but the mystery at the heart of the universe. The essence of the resurrection is that it is profound to the point of absolute simplicity. And so one of the best responses we can make to the mystery of the resurrection of Christ and the mystery of our own resurrection—our share in his resurrection—is to pray from a faith-filled heart an Our Father, ten Hail Marys, and a Glory Be. In other words, we are well advised to pray as much from the heart as from the head—which is why the Rosary is so perfect.

2. The Ascension: Authentic Faith Keeps Us Focused on the Here and Now

Fruit of the Mystery: Hope

After his suffering [Jesus] presented himself alive to [the apostles] by many convincing proofs, appearing to them during forty days and speaking about the kingdom of God. While staying with them, he ordered them not to leave Jerusalem, but to wait there for the promise of the Father. "This," he said, "is what you have heard from me; for John baptized with water, but you will be baptized with the Holy Spirit not many days from now."

So when they had come together, they asked him, "Lord, is this the time when you will restore the kingdom to Israel?" He replied, "It is not for you to know the times or periods that the Father has set by his own authority. But you will receive power when the Holy Spirit has come upon you; and you will be my witnesses in Jerusalem, in all Judea and Samaria, and to the ends of the earth." When he had said this, as they were watching, he was lifted up, and a cloud took him out of their sight. While he was going and they were gazing up toward heaven, suddenly two men in white robes stood by them. They said, "Men of Galilee, why do you stand looking up toward heaven? This Jesus, who has been taken up from you into heaven, will come in the same way as you saw him go into heaven."

—Acts 1:3-11

The most detailed account that exists for the second glorious mystery appears in the Acts of the Apostles. We live, of course, in the era of space exploration, and we need to recognize that the traditional presentation of the ascension of Jesus into heaven relies on an archaic cosmology, or understanding of the universe, where heaven was literally "up." Our interpretation of the ascension narrative must fit our modern understanding of how the universe is structured.

The point is not that Jesus "ascended" into heaven, literally, as much as that he made the transition from earth into the mystery of God's loving presence, to which the word "heaven" refers. When the Acts of the Apostles states that Jesus "was lifted up, and a cloud took him out of their sight," we need to be open to the likelihood that we're reading metaphors meant to communicate the truth that Jesus truly did "go," as it were, from this world to the mystery called "heaven." Also, we need to understand that heaven isn't a place; rather, heaven is, more accurately, a state of being.

The other truth communicated by this account is that Jesus made the transition from earth to heaven under his own power, so to speak. Whereas Mary (as we shall see) was "assumed" by God into heaven, Jesus "ascended" himself, with no need of his Father's assistance.

Some theologians suggest that the resurrection and ascension of Jesus are actually two facets of the same event, with some passage of time between the two. Be this as it may, the author of the Gospel of Luke and the Acts of the Apostles—scholarly consensus attributes both documents to the same source—clearly believed that it was important to describe the two events separately.

One lesson we can learn from this mystery of the Rosary is that our destiny, like that of Jesus, is not of this world. Rather, we are destined, from the moment of our creation, for bigger things that are beyond space and time. Just as Jesus "ascended" from this world, so we will pass from this world into heaven—again, whatever that may mean. In the meantime, however, we are called to focus on this world. We are not to stand around looking "up" to heaven. We are to live a life dedicated, day in and day out, to the loving service of God and neighbor.

3. The Descent of the Holy Spirit: Authentic Faith Is Open to the Holy Spirit in All Times and Places

Fruit of the Mystery: Love of God

> When the day of Pentecost had come, they were all together in one place. And suddenly from heaven there came a sound like the rush of a violent wind, and it filled the entire house where they were sitting. Divided tongues, as of fire, appeared among them, and a tongue rested on each of them. All of them were filled with the Holy Spirit and began to speak in other languages, as the Spirit gave them ability.
>
> —Acts 2:1-4

We rely for this mystery entirely upon a single New Testament account in the Acts of the Apostles. Acts 1:14 includes "Mary the mother of Jesus" among those who, after the ascension of Jesus, "were constantly devoting themselves to prayer."

Christians naturally assume, therefore, that Mary was among those who "were all together in one place" for the descent of the Holy Spirit on the first Pentecost.

Whether this narrative is meant to be taken as a literal account of events witnessed by everyone present, or whether Luke, the author of the Acts of the Apostles, used symbolic and metaphorical language to express the truth of a shared faith experience is largely unimportant. Either way, the point is that a profound transformation took place among the first followers of Jesus that could only be attributed to the activity and grace of God.

From this point on, the disciples have the courage and authority to proclaim the gospel and call others into loving intimacy with the risen Lord and with the community of his followers, the Church. Chapter 2 of Acts concludes with a description of a life of shared faith that Christian communities have held as an ideal ever since:

> All who believed were together and had all things in common; they would sell their possessions and goods and distribute the proceeds to all, as any had need. Day by day, as they spent much time together in the temple, they broke bread at home and ate their food with glad and generous hearts, praising God and having the goodwill of all the people. And day by day the Lord added to their number those who were being saved. (Acts 2:44-47)

Again, whether or not this is a literal historical description is unimportant. What matters is that it is a clear statement of the belief of the author of Luke and Acts—and presumably, the faith community he wrote for—that faith needs to be much more than a private, personal matter. Authentic Christian faith can't help but have an impact on a believer's lifestyle choices. Also, any who request membership in the community of faith do so in response to the presence and beckoning of Christ. Therefore, we who welcome them had better be careful about taking any credit for ourselves.

4. The Assumption of Mary: Authentic Faith Looks Forward to Having a Glorified Body

Fruit of the Mystery: Grace of a Happy Death

> We pronounce, declare, and define it to be a divinely revealed dogma: that the Immaculate Mother of God, the ever Virgin Mary, having completed the course of her earthly life, was assumed body and soul into heavenly glory.
>
> —Pope Pius XII, *Munificentissimus Deus*, 44

Pope Pius XII promulgated his declaration on the assumption of Mary, "body and soul" into heaven, on November 1, 1950. He chose to say nothing about whether Mary first experienced natural death. Regardless, the first thing we need to understand about this doctrine is that it was not a recent development. Belief among Christians in the assumption of the Blessed Virgin Mary goes back to at least the third century, and while none of the New Testament documents mention this event explicitly—or even mention belief in this event—it is by no means inconsistent with Scripture and is even consistent with deep scriptural themes.

The first known analysis of the assumption was written by Theoteknos, a sixth-century bishop of Jericho. His argument went like this: since the Old Testament tells us that Elijah ascended (1 Maccabees 2:58) and Revelation 21:14 clearly implies that a place in heaven was prepared for the apostles, so much more likely is it that Mary, the virgin mother of Jesus, must have been assumed into heaven to a place prepared for her.

Belief in this doctrine developed, for the most part, through sermons and devotional literature, which suggested that in view of her mission as the *Theotokos*, Mother of God, it made sense that Mary experienced death but not that her body would return to the earth. She gave physical life to Christ, so it was appropriate that he would give eternal life to her body. From the thirteenth century onward, theologians such as St. Thomas Aquinas and St. Bonaventure declared that belief in the assumption of Mary was a valid belief. It is also noteworthy that the Orthodox and Eastern churches, too, have always recognized the assumption of Mary.

In other words, when Pius XII declared the assumption of Mary to be a dogma of the Catholic Church, he gave the official stamp of approval to a belief that had ancient origins and had been around for many, many centuries as a part of the Church's sacred Tradition. Just as Tradition gave birth to the New Testament, so Tradition gave birth to the doctrine of the assumption of Mary. This particular glorious mystery reminds us both of Mary's assumption into heaven and of the important role of Tradition in the ongoing life of the Church.

It is also worth noting that the great twentieth-century German psychologist Carl Jung, although not a Christian, was delighted when he learned of Pope Pius XII's declaration. He stated publicly that the doctrine of the assumption reflected the Catholic Church's acceptance and appreciation for the physical world.

In a very real sense, the doctrine of the assumption of Mary celebrates the destiny that all the faithful will experience—that is, an existence of risen glory. Mary shared in the destiny of the risen Christ, just as we all will. But by virtue of her special role in the history of salvation, Mary experienced the fullness of the risen life immediately upon the conclusion of her earthly existence.

5. The Coronation of Mary as Queen of Heaven: Authentic Faith Looks to Mary as a Model

Fruit of the Mystery: Trust in Mary's Intercession

From the ancient Christian documents, from prayers of the liturgy, from the innate piety of the Christian people, from works of art, from every side we have gathered witnesses to the regal dignity of the Virgin Mother of God; we have likewise shown that the arguments deduced by Sacred Theology from the treasure store of the faith fully confirm this truth. Such a wealth of witnesses makes up a resounding chorus which changes the sublimity of the royal dignity of the Mother of God and of men, to whom every creature is subject, who is "exalted to the heavenly throne, above the choirs of angels" [Roman Brievary, Feast of the Assumption of the Blessed Virgin Mary].

—Pope Pius XII, *Ad Caeli Reginam*, 46

This mystery has been a part of the Rosary since at least the twelfth century. In 1954 Pope Pius XII added to the Church's calendar the feast of the Queenship of the Blessed Virgin Mary. The original date selected for this feast was May 31, but it was later moved to August 22, a week after the feast of the Assumption. This memorial celebrates the event that is highlighted by the fifth glorious mystery of the Rosary. From a devotional perspective, it is because of Jesus' close relationship with his mother and the role she played in our salvation that she also shares in his kingship.

Christians and Church documents have referred to Mary as "queen" since the fourth century. Various songs, litanies, and prayers also have called Mary "queen." The Church has attributed the title of "queen" to Mary in modern times through official documents, such as the Second Vatican Council's Constitution on the Church, *Lumen Gentium*: "And exalted by the Lord as Queen over all things, that she might be the more fully conformed to her Son" (59)[15]; and the 1954 encyclical of Pope Pius XII quoted above, *Ad Caeli Reginam*: "She is crowned in heavenly blessedness with the glory of a Queen" (1).

Once again, the Rosary includes among the mysteries an insight from sacred Tradition upon which it invites us to meditate. While the mystery of the assumption of Mary is an official Church doctrine, solemnly established as such by an infallible papal decree, the mystery of the coronation of Mary remains firmly rooted in Church documents and devotional practice as another way to venerate and honor the Blessed Virgin Mary.

What can we learn from reflecting on this mystery? Perhaps its main purpose is to remind us of the great dignity of Mary. Her son is King of heaven, and so, in virtue of her special and unique role as the mother of the Lord, we call her Queen of Heaven. It's as simple and as profound as that.

The Luminous Mysteries

Now prayed on Thursdays

The luminous mysteries, sometimes called the mysteries of light, are the most recently added to the Rosary. Pope St. John Paul II, in his 2002 apostolic letter *Rosarium Virginis Mariae,* pointed out that these five mysteries all come from the public ministry of Jesus in the Gospels. In explaining his theological rationale for adding mysteries to the Rosary—the first time anyone had done so in many centuries—Pope St. John Paul II wrote that the mystery of Christ as a whole is a mystery of light. Indeed, the Gospel of John refers to Jesus as the "light of the world" (8:12). The pope explained:

> This truth emerges in a special way during the years of his public life, when he proclaims the Gospel of the Kingdom. In proposing to the Christian community five significant moments—"luminous" mysteries—during this phase of Christ's life, I think that the following can be fittingly singled out: (1) his Baptism in the Jordan, (2) his self-manifestation at the wedding of Cana, (3) his proclamation of the Kingdom of God, with his call to conversion, (4) his Transfiguration, and finally, (5) his institution of the Eucharist, as the sacramental expression of the Paschal Mystery. Each of these mysteries is *a revelation of the Kingdom now present in the very person of Jesus.* (*Rosarium Virginis Mariae,* 21)

Although the Holy Father did not point this out, it is noteworthy too that the events upon which the luminous mysteries focus are all major events in the Gospels that had previously not been part of the Rosary. The addition of these "new" Rosary mysteries brings a greater balance to the Rosary and a more complete awareness of the public ministry of Jesus to those who pray the Rosary. By drawing the luminous mysteries from events in the Gospels, Pope St. John Paul II also reminded the world of the centrality of the Gospels as sources for any form of Christian prayer or devotion.

1. The Baptism of Jesus: Authentic Faith Is Rooted in the Grace of Baptism

Fruit of the Mystery: Openness to the Holy Spirit

Then Jesus came from Galilee to John at the Jordan, to be baptized by him. John would have prevented him, saying, "I need to be baptized by you, and do you come to me?" But Jesus answered him, "Let it be so now; for it is proper for us in this way to fulfill all righteousness." Then he consented. And when Jesus had been baptized, just as he came up from the water, suddenly the heavens were opened to him and he saw the Spirit of God descending like a dove and alighting on him. And a voice form heaven said, "This is my Son, the Beloved, with whom I am well pleased."

—Matthew 3:13-17

In his apostolic letter *Rosarium Virginis Mariae*, Pope St. John Paul II reflected briefly on each of the new luminous mysteries. Although it may not seem particularly significant at first glance, in each case where the event recalled by a mystery occurs in two or more Gospels, the pope explicitly referred to this fact by adding to the reference of the chapter and verse the words "and parallels." For example, his reference to this first luminous mystery reads, "cf. Matthew 3:17 and parallels" (21). In other words, the Holy Father drew attention to the fact that there are other baptism-in-the-Jordan narratives in addition to the one in Matthew, each with its own theological perspective.

The pope acknowledged this in a matter-of-fact way, in passing; but in doing so, he reflected the mature Catholic understanding of the Scriptures and the whole modern history of Catholic Scripture scholarship, including its various scientific and historical methods of interpretation. Not only does the pope affirm the modern history of Catholic Scripture scholarship, but by his own example, he reminds all Catholics that there is nothing helpful about a naive, simplistic, or overly literal approach to the Bible. The same is true for the Rosary, which—it should be clear by now—is deeply rooted in the Scriptures through its mysteries and prayers.

One unique characteristic of Matthew's baptism-in-the-Jordan narrative is that it alone includes the interaction and dialogue between Jesus and John the Baptist. Of particular significance for Matthew's Jewish Christian audience is John's open acknowledgment of Jesus' superiority. At the same time, it is significant that Jesus gently rebuffs John's objection. Jesus had no objection to accepting John's baptism, for to do so was to "fulfill all righteousness." In Matthew's Gospel, this phrase refers to fulfilling prophecy and acting according to the requirements of moral conduct according to God's will. In other words, in Matthew's Gospel, Jesus wants to act in accord with his Jewish roots.

In Mark and Luke, as well as in Matthew, the Spirit descends like a dove, and God's voice from heaven announces Jesus' divine sonship and reveals his Father's approval of him. Notice that Matthew says that "the heavens were opened to him," which suggests that only Jesus witnessed this phenomenon and, by extension, that only he heard the voice of God speaking. Yet the Gospel of John indicates that John the Baptist at least saw "the Spirit descending from heaven like a dove . . . on him" (John 1:32).

Of course, one important purpose of the baptism-in-the-Jordan narratives in all three synoptic accounts is to witness to Jesus' deepest identity, that is, that he is the Son of God, with whom God is "well pleased." That much is common to Matthew, Mark, and Luke. As we pray this mystery of the Rosary, it reminds us of Jesus' divinity in a world where many do not believe that Jesus is divine.

At the same time, we may remind ourselves that, in the Gospels, context is always significant. The verses that come before and after any given saying or parable of Jesus, for example, affect how we understand that saying or parable. In Matthew's Gospel, the baptism of Jesus segues right into the temptation of Jesus in the desert. In effect, Matthew follows up an affirmation of Jesus' divinity with an affirmation of his humanity.

Sometimes believers tend to neglect this balance in their attitude toward Jesus, overlooking or downplaying his humanity in favor of his divinity. In a secularized culture, however, the opposite is more common: people think of Jesus as just "a good man." In such a cultural context, therefore, it's good that the first of the luminous mysteries reminds us of Jesus' divinity.

2. The Wedding at Cana: Authentic Faith Takes All Worries and Concerns to Christ

Fruit of the Mystery: To Jesus through Mary

On the third day there was a wedding in Cana of Galilee, and the mother of Jesus was there. Jesus and his disciples had also been invited to the wedding. When the wine gave out, the mother of Jesus said to him, "They have no wine." And Jesus said to her, "Woman, what concern is that to you and to me? My hour has not yet come." His mother said to the servants, "Do whatever he tells you." Now standing there were six stone water jars for the Jewish rites of purification, each holding twenty or thirty gallons. Jesus said to them, "Fill the jars with water." And they filled them up to the brim. He said to them, "Now draw some out, and take it to the chief steward." So they took it. When the steward tasted the water that had become wine, and did not know where it came from (though the servants who had drawn the water knew), the steward called the bridegroom and said to him, "Everyone serves the good wine first, and then the inferior wine after the guests have become drunk. But you have kept the good wine until now." Jesus did this, the first of his signs, in Cana of Galilee, and revealed his glory; and his disciples believed in him.

—John 2:1-11

This second luminous mystery occurs only in the Gospel of John. As we noted earlier, one of the dominant characteristics of the fourth Gospel is the way that it emphasizes and highlights the divinity of Jesus—even though it also leaves no doubt about Jesus' complete humanity. This conviction about Jesus' divinity shows itself in this luminous mystery, when Jesus causes water to become high-quality wine. But there is much more that goes on in this wonderful narrative, and if we overlook it, we deprive ourselves of many spiritual benefits.

Notice that the first person mentioned in the narrative is not Jesus but "the mother of Jesus." The Gospel then adds—as if it were an afterthought—that "Jesus and his disciples had also been invited to the wedding." The reader can't help but conclude that the main character in this narrative is Mary. Can anyone read this familiar story and not feel compelled to admit that the faith community from which it came had a special place in its heart for the mother of Jesus?

It is noteworthy, of course, that the fourth Gospel never refers to the mother of Jesus by her name. Any explanation for this must remain in the realm of conjecture, but it doesn't seem unreasonable to suggest that perhaps the reason for not calling Mary by her name is that she was like a mother in the community of faith in which the Gospel of John developed. Just as a woman's children in our own time and culture are not likely to refer to her by her name, so perhaps, in the community of John's Gospel, the mother of Jesus was so beloved, and her presence so respected, that no one would ever call her by her name, especially in the third person. People would always think of and refer to her in terms of her relationship with the Lord.

Only the community of the fourth Gospel preserved and passed down the story of the wedding at Cana. Perhaps this was because the account of this event came from Mary herself. And perhaps the community of the fourth Gospel preserved the memory of this event because—as John 19:26-27 implies—Mary stayed with John, "the beloved disciple," from the day of Jesus' crucifixion until the end of her earthly life. To repeat, this is all conjecture, but it's a reasonable possibility.

To return to our narrative, the interaction between the main characters (the mother of Jesus, Jesus himself, and his disciples) and the context (a wedding) results in some delightful and sometimes amazing insights. At the same time, it's important to not read into the narrative romantic or pious interpretations that the text simply doesn't support.

Without giving any prelude or description of the setting, the Gospel simply says, "When the wine gave out . . . " It's almost as if it was common at weddings in Jesus' time and culture, or at least not unusual, for the wine supply to run out. Regardless, the main character in the story—"the mother of Jesus"— notices this problem and informs Jesus about it: "They have no wine."

Jesus' response is the first-century Palestinian equivalent of "Mother! What do you expect me to do about it?" Then, however, Jesus adds words—"My hour has not yet come"—that have no modern equivalent, so we find it difficult to understand what he means. Perhaps he didn't feel that the time was right to begin his public ministry. And although it may strike modern ears as disrespectful for Jesus to address his mother as "Woman," this was a normal, polite custom, so we shouldn't attribute anything negative to it.

Some Catholic Scripture scholars suggest that Jesus and the Gospel of John want to show by these words that Jesus didn't go around causing miracles to happen for frivolous reasons, even for the sake of friends and family, contrary to the fanciful miracle stories in many of the apocryphal gospels. These so-called gospels were never accepted by the Christian faith community as divinely inspired.

The narrative continues with "his mother" apparently ignoring or overlooking Jesus' response. Addressing the servants without speaking to Jesus, Mary turns the whole situation over to him. "Do whatever he tells you," she says to the servants. This is the crucial moment in the narrative.

John's Gospel says nothing about why "the mother of Jesus" presents Jesus with the fact that the wine supply has been exhausted. She just does so. The Gospel also does not tell us why his mother ignores Jesus' initial response. Again, we are left to our conjectures.

Perhaps Mary's response to Jesus' words comes from her confidence that he will act on her compassionate concern for the newlywed couple, no matter what his personal inclination might be. Indeed, that appears to be the case, for once Mary tells the servants to do whatever he tells them, Jesus acts on his mother's concerns, rather than according to his own apparent preferences, by causing the water in six twenty-to-thirty-gallon jars to become fine wine. The Gospel comments that this was "the first of his signs," for the fourth Gospel never uses the word "miracle" to describe such events. Rather, they are "signs," the primary purpose of which is to reveal Jesus' "glory," that is, his divine nature, and to bring to faith those who witness these "signs."

Meditating on this event in the context of the Rosary, we come to know more about who Mary is, about who Jesus is, and about the nature of their relationship with each other— not only then but now. The Gospel of John is clear about this: "the mother of Jesus" has influence with her son. Although he may be inclined one way, she can incline him another way. In the Cana wedding narrative, Mary actually seems to bring to her son's attention the need to act with compassion when he is not thinking of the need to do so.

None of the Gospels include a narrative of the wedding of Mary and Joseph. Who knows what memories Mary had from her own nuptials? She could empathize with the young couple, whereas Jesus showed no sign of doing so. Sometimes a mother needs to step in and use her influence.

Traditionally, prayer to Mary for her intercession takes this insight seriously. Perhaps—countless numbers of Catholics down through the centuries supposed—the Lord still can be influenced by his mother when he might not otherwise be inclined to help. Some might wonder about this presumption: after all, the post-resurrection Church must take for granted not the Jesus of first-century Palestine—who, on occasions before his public ministry began, such as this one, may have been a bit slow on the uptake—but the risen Christ. Still, the mother-son relationship is a part of the heavenly condition that both Jesus and Mary enjoy. So praying to Mary to intercede with Jesus for us and our concerns seems natural and understandable. Indeed, this perspective is fundamental to the Rosary.

3. The Proclamation of the Kingdom: Authentic Faith Experiences God's Kingdom Now and Anticipates the Kingdom to Come

Fruit of the Mystery: Repentance and Trust in God

> [Jesus said,] "The time is fulfilled, and the kingdom of God has come near; repent, and believe in the good news."
> —Mark 1:15

This third luminous mystery fills a significant gap in the echoing of the gospel that the Rosary was always supposed to do. The consensus among both Catholic and mainline Protestant New Testament scholars is that these words of Jesus, from early in the oldest of the four Gospels, gather into a nutshell the heart of Jesus' message. If you want to know the foundation of all of Jesus' preaching, teaching, and actions, you get it in this one sentence.

The problem for us in the twenty-first century, of course, is that this one sentence is not so easy for us to comprehend. We need to make a little effort to figure out its meaning. When we do that, however, we begin to understand just how earthshaking and life changing the gospel really is.

Let's take it one phrase at a time:

"The time is fulfilled, . . ." These words resonated with meaning for Mark's first audience, for they knew what it meant to wait for so long for the coming of the Messiah. Nothing could have been more exciting than the announcement that the time of waiting was over.

"*. . . and the kingdom of God has come near . . .*" The Greek phrase for "kingdom of God" is *basileia tou theou,* and it is a far more dynamic idea than our geographical notion of a kingdom. Sometimes the phrase is translated "reign of God," an attempt to inject into the translation some of the dynamic, active meaning of the Greek phrase. To say that the *basileia tou theou* "has come near" is to say that the personal presence of God and his infinite love have begun to permeate the universe and transform all things.

In Jesus, God's own personal self is near in a completely new way. Indeed, Jesus is the most complete manifestation possible of God's own self in history, in time and space. To speak of the *basileia tou theou* is to give the Incarnation cosmic dimensions. Now the love of God is breaking into creation in a way that is beginning to transform all things.

It is important to notice, however, the phrase "has come near." Jesus does not say that the *basileia tou theou* is present totally and completely, here and now. Rather, his words must be understood to announce the *beginning* or the *coming* of the kingdom of God, not its final accomplishment. Thus, Scripture scholars refer to what they call the already-but-not-yet character of the kingdom of God in time and space. Yes, the kingdom or reign of God is near and beginning to transform everything. But obviously, the final consummation of all things in Christ has not yet been completed.

"*. . . repent, . . .*" Who has never seen a sign along the side of a road urging everyone, "Repent!" The "repentance" that those who post such signs have in mind is most likely straightforward: you should put your evil ways behind you and start living by the Ten Commandments. But the word in the Greek New Testament that is behind English words such as "repentance" is *metanoia,* and it means far more than to "give up drinkin' and cussin' and start goin' to church on Sunday."

Metanoia refers to being transformed by adopting a whole new way of looking at life and the universe. If you are going in one direction, you need to turn around and go in the opposite direction. From now on, your perspective on yourself, your lifestyle, and your relationships with others and with the earth, our home, must be that of Christ.

Repentance means changing your lifestyle from the ground up. To paraphrase words from the Gospel of John, *metanoia* means living in and on behalf of the world but not according to the values and ideals of the world—insofar as the world rejects the most basic values, ideals, and goals of the gospel (see John 17). In other words, repentance is not for the faint of heart, and it's a lifelong project.

Also, true Christian faith is not merely a source of comfort and reassurance. It is that, of course. But the comfort of the gospel cannot be separated from the challenges and demands of the gospel. As an old saying puts it, the gospel of Christ, to be real, must comfort the afflicted and afflict the comfortable. And if you're living in just about any of the so-called developed Western nations, believe me, you are probably among the comfortable that the gospel of Christ should afflict.

At this point, to pay close attention to where our line of thought has been going is to find ourselves puzzling over the word "gospel," which we will need to sort out in order to understand the next phrase:

". . . and believe in the good news." The Greek word *evangelion,* which is sometimes translated "gospel" and sometimes translated "good news," is, like so many words in the New Testament, not easy to translate into English. Old translations sometimes used "glad tidings," which is quaint and not particularly helpful to understanding what *evangelion* really means. The "gospel," or "good news," refers to a reality that we understand incompletely, at best. What exactly is this "good news"?

At its most basic level, "gospel" refers to the news about the reality of God's love for us and for all creation, which is unconditional in the sense that our Father never withholds his love as long as we are open to receiving it. The good news about God's love for us, both collectively and individually, is inseparable from the announcement of Jesus about the arrival, already but not yet, of the kingdom or reign of God—for they are one and the same reality. The kingdom of God is our Father's loving presence permeating, healing, and rescuing all. This is also the message of salvation and the news about our redemption. These are all ways of talking about the same reality—namely, God's love for us and its healing and saving effects.

Moreover, understanding and accepting this gospel are what motivate the *metanoia,* the conversion or repentance that we discussed above. The only appropriate response to the gospel is to turn away from self in order to focus more on God and neighbor.

In the context of the Rosary, this mystery reminds us of God's infinite love, which arrives and is arriving in the coming of his reign or kingdom. Consequently, this mystery is meant to touch our hearts and reinvigorate our dedication to living the fullness of the Christian life, a life centered not on self but on God and others.

4. The Transfiguration: Authentic Faith Is Aware of Its Roots

Fruit of the Mystery: Desire for Holiness

> Six days later, Jesus took with him Peter and James and John, and led them up a high mountain apart, by themselves. And he was transfigured before them, and his clothes became dazzling white, such as no one on earth could bleach them. And there appeared to them Elijah with Moses, who were talking with Jesus. Then Peter said to Jesus, "Rabbi, it is good for us to be here; let us make three dwellings, one for you, one for Moses, and one for Elijah." He did not know what to say, for they were terrified. Then a cloud overshadowed them, and from the cloud there came a voice, "This is my Son, the Beloved; listen to him!" Suddenly when they looked around, they saw no one with them any more, but only Jesus.
>
> —Mark 9:2-8

If any of the mysteries of the Rosary deserve to be called "luminous," the transfiguration of Christ certainly does. This event, which appears in slightly different forms in the Gospels of Matthew, Mark, and Luke, is an astonishing experience that Jesus shared with Peter, James, and John. Some parts of the narrative have perplexed generations of Gospel scholars. For example, what is the point of Peter's apparently senseless remarks about wanting to set up "three dwellings"? Endless pious suggestions and guesses have been made about the meaning of these words.

Essentially, this narrative reveals Jesus' deepest identity as the Son of God. The apostles hear a second time the words "This is my Son, the Beloved; listen to him!" which God proclaimed at Jesus' baptism in the Jordan. The narrative also relates Jesus to Moses and Elijah, two of the greatest Old Testament figures, making Jesus the fulfillment of everything taught by these two ancient personages and more. For a brief moment, Peter, James, and John get a glimpse of Jesus in his final glory. One wonders if they reflected on this moment in the difficult days following Jesus' death.

As a mystery of the Rosary, the transfiguration event is a reminder of Jesus' divinity and of our own relationship with Judaism through the Old Testament. We may find ourselves wanting to learn more about the Judaism from which Christianity emerged. And in difficult times, we can try to remember that Jesus has promised us a share in his glory too.

5. The Institution of the Eucharist: Authentic Faith Is Devoted to the Eucharist

Fruit of the Mystery: Adoration

For I received from the Lord what I also handed on to you, that the Lord Jesus on the night when he was betrayed took a loaf of bread, and when he had given thanks, he broke it and said, "This is my body that is for you. Do

> this in remembrance of me." In the same way he took the cup also, after supper, saying, "This cup is the new covenant in my blood. Do this, as often as you drink it, in remembrance of me."
>
> —1 Corinthians 11:23-25

The last of the luminous mysteries is particularly significant for Catholics, for whom the Eucharist carries such profound meaning. There are four accounts of this mystery in the New Testament, one in each of the Gospels of Matthew, Mark, and Luke and one in St. Paul's First Letter to the Corinthians. In fact, the institution narrative in 1 Corinthians is the oldest we have, since Scripture scholars date this letter at about twenty years before the oldest Gospel, that of Mark.

This luminous mystery affords a rich opportunity for us to deepen our appreciation for the Sacrament of the Eucharist by focusing on the meaning of the words Jesus used at the Last Supper.

Catholics are familiar with the traditional words of institution used in the Mass, words that come directly from the New Testament accounts of the Last Supper. Taking the bread, Jesus says that it is his body; and taking the cup of wine, he says that the wine is his blood. We can gain a great deal by understanding that in Jesus' time, the phrase "body and blood" was a Semitic way of saying what we would say today with words such as "whole self." In essence, Jesus' words mean, "This bread and wine are my whole (risen) self."

Catholics have understood this reality for a long time. Following the Counter-Reformation Council of Trent, in the mid-sixteenth century, only the priest received Communion from the chalice; everyone else was limited to consuming the consecrated bread. Still, all understood that the "whole person" of the risen Christ was present in the consecrated bread.

Even today, when a person is ill and unable to swallow the consecrated host, he or she may be given a few drops of only the consecrated wine for Communion. To receive either bread or wine or both is to receive the whole Christ, "body and blood, soul and divinity," to use the traditional phrase.

Here is another insight. As we noted above in passing, when it comes to understanding the Eucharist, we need to take seriously that the Eucharist is an opportunity to be with the Lord Jesus as he is now—that is, in his *risen* state. It is the risen Lord who is present in our midst when we celebrate the Eucharist, and it is the risen Lord we receive in Holy Communion. The Mass is not some mysterious, sacramental "blast from the past." Rather, the risen Lord is present among us now, and it is the whole person of the risen Christ that we receive in Holy Communion.

In other words, there is an intimate connection between the mystery of the resurrection, the mystery of the Eucharist, and the real presence of Christ in the consecrated bread and wine. To use the word "resurrection" doesn't make everything crystal clear, however. Rather, it only compounds the mystery.

When we gather to celebrate the Eucharist, it is the risen Christ in our midst. And when we receive Holy Communion, it is the risen Christ we receive. But what does "risen" mean? We don't know, but whatever it means, there is an intimate link between "resurrection" and "eternal life."

We know that "resurrected" does not mean merely "resuscitated," and we know that "eternal" is not a word for "endless," but that's about all we do know. We know what "eternal" and "resurrection" are not. Perhaps the most accurate positive comment we can make about these two words is that they both describe the intimacy with our loving Father that we begin to experience here and now, in time and space, and that becomes complete only on the other side of natural death. To receive the whole person of the risen Christ in Holy Communion is, in fact, to receive the beginning of one's ultimate destiny, namely heaven—whatever *that* word means!

It is wonderful that, with the addition of the luminous mysteries to the Rosary by Pope St. John Paul II, this centuries-old prayer now includes a meditation upon and a reminder of the tremendous blessing of the Eucharist. What an unmatchable gift! Each time we pray the luminous mysteries, we are reminded of the depth, breadth, and height of the love of Christ for all of us, present in every breath we take and every beat of our heart and present in a special way every time we participate in the Mass and receive Holy Communion. What a tremendous privilege it is to participate in the Mass!

CHAPTER 5

GETTING DOWN TO BASICS

How to Pray the Rosary

If you've never prayed the Rosary before, this chapter will give you the basics; and if you're returning to the Rosary after a long time away, you can use this chapter as a "refresher course." Keep in mind, however, that there are no "Rosary police" checking up on you, to make sure that you're doing it "the right way." In the long run, you may pray the Rosary however you prefer to pray it.

The main objective of the Rosary is the same as that of any prayer—to nourish your intimacy with the triune God and with the communion of saints in this world and the next. So whatever serves that purpose is good.

If you want to pray the Rosary in the customary manner, however, there is a traditional way to go about it. The prayers of the Rosary are provided here, in case you don't already know them.

Because praying the Rosary involves repetitive prayer, it's a good idea to have a rosary. If you don't have a religious goods store in your area, you can find several sources on the Internet—some of which even offer free rosaries.

There are two basic ways to pray the Rosary—alone or with one or more people. If you pray the Rosary with others, the custom is for one person to lead the group, primarily by

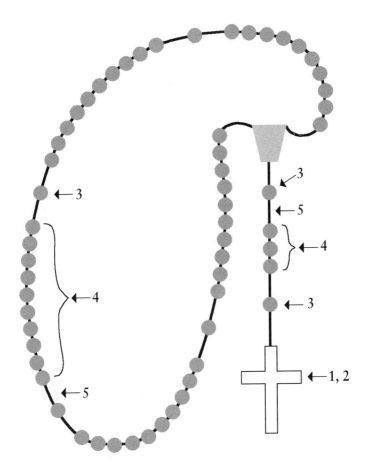

1. The Sign of the Cross
2. The Apostles' Creed
3. The Our Father
4. The Hail Mary
5. The Glory Be

saying the first half of each prayer and announcing each of the mysteries.

For simplicity's sake, we'll assume here that you are praying the Rosary by yourself. If you join a group, most likely many of those present will understand how to pray the Rosary as a group, so all you'll need to do is follow along. When praying the Rosary alone, you may either recite the prayers aloud or say them silently—it's up to you.

A rosary consists of six Our Father beads and five decades (sets of ten) Hail Mary beads plus one set of three Hail Mary beads. The Apostles' Creed is said while holding the crucifix, and the Glory Be is said while holding the chain or knot after each set of Hail Marys. The Hail Holy Queen is said at the end of the Rosary. Here's how to go about it. You may be surprised when you see how easy it really is:

Make the Sign of the Cross

You begin the Rosary by making the Sign of the Cross using the small crucifix on the rosary. Simply hold the crucifix on your rosary with your fingers and touch it to your forehead, your chest, and then your left and right shoulders while saying,

> In the name of the Father [forehead], and of the Son [chest], and of the Holy [left shoulder] Spirit [right shoulder]. Amen.

Pray the Apostles' Creed
Still holding the crucifix, pray the Apostles' Creed:

I believe in God,
the Father almighty,
Creator of heaven and earth,
and in Jesus Christ, his only Son, our Lord,
who was conceived by the Holy Spirit,
born of the Virgin Mary,
suffered under Pontius Pilate,
was crucified, died and was buried;
he descended into hell;
on the third day he rose again from the dead;
he ascended into heaven,
and is seated at the right hand of God the Father almighty;
from there he will come to judge the living and the dead.

I believe in the Holy Spirit,
the holy catholic Church,
the communion of saints,
the forgiveness of sins,
the resurrection of the body,
and life everlasting.
Amen.

Pray the Our Father

Holding the first bead of your rosary (the bead closest to the crucifix), pray the Our Father:

Our Father, who art in heaven,
hallowed be thy name;
thy kingdom come;
thy will be done on earth as it is in heaven.
Give us this day our daily bread;
and forgive us our trespasses
as we forgive those who trespass
against us;
and lead us not into temptation,
but deliver us from evil. Amen.

(If you came, or are coming, to Catholicism from a Protestant tradition, remember that Catholics conclude the Our Father as written here. Catholics use the doxology—"For the kingdom, the power and the glory are yours, now and forever"— only in the context of the Mass, and then it is separated from the Our Father by a prayer said by the priest.)

Pray Three Hail Marys

Hold each of the three beads in the next series one at a time, and pray a Hail Mary for each bead:

Hail Mary, full of grace,
the Lord is with thee/you;
blessed art thou/are you among women,
and blessed is the fruit of thy/your womb, Jesus.
Holy Mary, Mother of God, pray for us sinners
now and at the hour of our death. Amen.

Pray the Glory Be

Holding the chain or knot that comes after the series of three Hail Mary beads, pray the Glory Be:

Glory be to the Father, the Son, and the Holy Spirit; as it was in the beginning, is now, and ever shall be, world without end. Amen.

If you like, you can say the following after each Glory Be:

O my Jesus, forgive us our sins, save us from the fires of hell, and lead all souls to heaven, especially those in most need of thy (your) mercy. Amen.

It's up to you whether you use this prayer, or not. Some Catholics wouldn't pray the Rosary without it; others don't care for it. If it appeals to you, go ahead and say it. If not, skip it.

Say the Five Decades

The next set of prayers—consisting of an Our Father, ten Hail Marys, and a Glory Be—is repeated five times, once for each mystery of the Rosary. While holding the next single bead, announce the first mystery you are praying today—joyful, sorrowful, glorious, or luminous. For example, "The first joyful mystery, the annunciation."

Theoretically, the idea is to meditate or reflect upon this mystery while praying an Our Father, ten Hail Marys, and a Glory Be. If you can do that, great. If not, don't worry about it.

Personally, I suspect that the repetitive nature of the Rosary actually short-circuits conscious reflection on anything—let alone a mystery of faith—and acts something like a mantra does in the meditation methods of Zen Buddhism. The Rosary gives the fingers and tongue something to do, so that your mind and heart can "go deep," as it were, in wordless prayer.

Indeed, Thomas Merton once remarked that he found it impossible to meditate on the mysteries while praying the Hail Marys. Instead, Merton said, he prayed each decade "in honor of" the mystery assigned to it.

After announcing the first mystery and still holding the single bead, pray the Our Father. For each of the ten beads in the first decade of the Rosary, say one Hail Mary. When you reach the chain or knot after the tenth Hail Mary bead, say one Glory Be. Then hold the next single bead, announce the next mystery, say an Our Father, say the next set of ten Hail Marys, and say another Glory Be. Do this until you finish all five decades.

Say the Hail Holy Queen or Salve Regina

When you have completed the fifth decade of the Rosary and said the final Glory Be, say the Hail Holy Queen:

Hail, holy Queen, mother of mercy,
our life, our sweetness, and our hope.
To you we cry, poor banished children of Eve;
to you we send up our sighs,
mourning and weeping in this valley of tears.
Turn, then, most gracious advocate,
your eyes of mercy toward us;
and after this, our exile,
show unto us the blessed fruit of your womb, Jesus.
O clement, O loving, O sweet Virgin Mary.

If you wish, you may also add this final verse-and-response prayer:

V: Pray for us, O holy Mother of God.
R: That we may be made worthy of the promises of Christ.

That's it. That's all there is to praying the Rosary. After you have prayed it a few times, you'll know how easy it is. The more you pray the Rosary, however, the deeper you'll get into it and the more you'll discover its spiritual riches.

APPENDIX A

PUTTING IT INTO PRACTICE

Making the Rosary Your Own

One of the beauties of the Rosary is that no two people are going to have exactly the same experience with it: it is a personal prayer that you can adapt to the individual circumstances of your life. You may decide to pray the Rosary as it has traditionally been prayed, without any variations. Or you may develop a fondness for a particular set of mysteries or even substitute your own meditations for the traditional mysteries.

You may decide to focus on cultivating the fruits of the mysteries while you pray, or you may find that you can't concentrate on anything other than the prayers themselves. You may use the Rosary at particular times of the day or in particular situations, and you may even fall asleep sometimes while you're praying it. And all of that is okay! You should feel free to make the Rosary your personal prayer of devotion.

There Is More Than One Way to Pray the Rosary

As noted early in this book, for the most part we limit ourselves here to the standard, conventional way to pray the

Rosary. Still, the Rosary is an adaptable prayer, and there are situations and circumstances in which it can be helpful to know of other ways to pray it. So here are a few.

The Scriptural Rosary

The scriptural character of the Rosary should be more than evident by now. Both the prayers of the Rosary and its mysteries, with few exceptions, come directly from the Gospels. The so-called scriptural Rosary adds brief passages from the Gospels to each mystery at the beginning of each decade or set of ten Hail Marys, or it adds a short passage from Scripture for *each* Hail Mary of every decade.

Chaplets

Consult a dictionary and you'll find that the word "chaplet" has different definitions. For our purposes here, "chaplet" refers to a personal devotional prayer that uses prayer beads, though not always the standard five-decade rosary. There are many different chaplets based on various devotions.

Possibly the most popular chaplet today is the Chaplet of Divine Mercy. Also called the Divine Mercy Chaplet, this prayer is centered on devotion to the mercy of God as revealed by Jesus to St. Faustina Kowalska (1905–1938). Faustina, known as "the apostle of mercy," was a Polish religious sister of the Congregation of the Sisters of Our Lady of Mercy. Pope St. John Paul II canonized her in 2000.

Faustina reported that she received the chaplet devotional through visions and conversations with Jesus, who made specific promises regarding the recitation of the prayers. He said this, for example: "The souls that say this chaplet will be embraced by My mercy during their lifetime and especially at the hour of their death." The Divine Mercy Chaplet is prayed on rosary beads but uses the prayers Jesus revealed to Faustina. These include the prayer on the ten beads of each decade: "For the sake of your sorrowful passion, have mercy on us and on the whole world." For more information, consult the website thedivinemercy.org.

The Anglican/Episcopalian Rosary

The Anglican Rosary is a contemplative prayer form. It is a fairly modern prayer combining the Roman Catholic Rosary with the Orthodox Jesus Prayer Rope. It is comprised of thirty-three beads (the traditional number of years of Jesus' life). There is one "invitatory" bead followed by four sets of seven beads each (called "weeks") with a single bead (called the "cruciform" bead) in between each week.

In the Judeo-Christian tradition, the number seven is that of spiritual perfection and completion. The circle of beads is prayed, unhurriedly, three times to signify the Holy Trinity. This makes for ninety-nine prayers, and in Middle Eastern traditions, ninety-nine is the complete number of the Divine Names. If you include a prayer on the cross, at the beginning or the end, this brings the total number of prayers said to one hundred, which represents the fullness of creation. Typically, the saying of the Rosary is followed by a period of silence for reflection.

There are no set prayers for the Anglican Rosary. It is your choice. The Book of Common Prayer brims with choices; particularly among the morning and evening prayers, the prayers of the people, the numerous collects, and even lectionary readings. Canticles and psalms are time-honored devotions, as are the Jesus Prayer, the Lord's Prayer, and the Serenity Prayer.

Remember, it is the practice that is important, the time spent in communion with God; the rosary is simply the vehicle for getting there.

[This material and additional information about the Anglican Rosary can be found at stmargaretilford.org.uk/anglican-rosary.]

A Protestant Rosary

Some Protestant denominations—including Lutherans, Presbyterians, and Baptists, as well as countless Christian sects—object strenuously to the Rosary. Many feel that it has overtones of Mariolotry and that the repetitive character of the Rosary seems inconsistent with Jesus' admonition against heaping up "empty phrases" (Matthew 6:7). Now and then, however, Protestants choose to pray the Rosary and find it both meaningful and rewarding.

In this case, as long as they are comfortable with praying the Hail Mary, the only potential obstacles are the fourth and fifth glorious mysteries, which have no direct connection with Scripture, namely, the Assumption of Mary into Heaven and the Coronation of Mary as Queen of Heaven. They may decide not to use the glorious mysteries at all, or they may substitute

two other events in Scripture for the assumption and coronation. Two possibilities are Jesus' Sermon on the Mount (Matthew 5:1-11) and Jesus' raising Lazarus to life (John 11:38-44).

The Fiat Rosary

Fiat is Latin for "let it be done." The reference here is to
Mary's response to the angel at the annunciation: "Here
am I, the servant of the Lord; let it be with me according
to your word" (Luke 1:38).

Veronica O'Brien (1905–1998), an Irish lay missionary,
reported that the Fiat Rosary was given to her in prayer on
September 7, 1984, the eve of the feast of the Nativity of
Mary. *The Hidden Hand of God,* by Belgian Cardinal Leon-
Joseph Suenens (1904–1996), includes O'Brien's description
of her experience:

> During the night I was saddened by the thought that although
> Mother's Day is becoming more and more popular, the Birthday
> of Mary, the Mother of all Mothers, would not be celebrated
> in Christian homes. In my prayers, I said to the Lord: "Jesus,
> tomorrow (September 8th) is the Feast of the Nativity of your
> Mother. Every child in the world gives his mother a present
> for her birthday. What will You give Your Mother, Jesus?"
> And suddenly, as a spiritual flash of light, I saw in my mind an
> image of a small, reduced rosary, and I heard the Lord say to
> me: "Here is my Birthday present to my Mother; it will help
> her to make me known to the very ends of the earth. Make it
> known all over the world."[16]

The Fiat Rosary

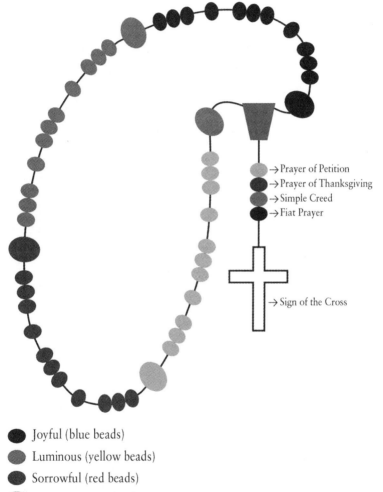

→ Prayer of Petition
→ Prayer of Thanksgiving
→ Simple Creed
→ Fiat Prayer

→ Sign of the Cross

Joyful (blue beads)
Luminous (yellow beads)
Sorrowful (red beads)
Glorious (white beads)

Veronica told Cardinal Suenens about her experience, and with permission from Pope St. John Paul II, together they worked to spread the Fiat Rosary. Cardinal Suenens, who had been a moderator of the Second Vatican Council, said, "May this little Rosary find its way into many homes, so that they may become cenacles of apostles, gathered around the Virgin Mary to receive the Spirit of Pentecost." [17]

This Rosary for our times is a simple way to pray the Rosary. It includes three of the joyful, three of the luminous, three of the sorrowful, and three of the glorious mysteries on one string of beads.

Although it isn't absolutely requisite, you'll find it much easier to pray this prayer if you use a Fiat rosary. You can order one from thefiatrosary.com. The Fiat rosary has four sets of beads, colored red, white, yellow, and blue.

Here are the instructions for praying the Fiat Rosary.

With the crucifix, make the Sign of the Cross:

In the name of the Father, and of the Son, and of the Holy Spirit. Amen.

On the *blue* bead closest to the crucifix, recite the Fiat Prayer (by Cardinal Suenens):

Most Holy Spirit, help me to relive, in union with Mary, the joyful, luminous, sorrowful, and glorious mysteries of Jesus. Grant that I may be inspired by the faith of my baptism, nourished by the Eucharist, and renewed in the grace of Pentecost, so as to live, in word and deed, always and everywhere, as a faithful witness of Christ and of the love of His Divine Heart. Amen.

On the *yellow* bead closest to the crucifix, recite this simple creed:

I believe in God the Father, Maker of our world so wide.
I believe in Jesus Christ, who for me was crucified.
I believe in the Holy Spirit, sent by God to be my guide.
I believe in the Catholic Church and all the saints in heaven too.
I know that God forgives my sins and helps me to begin anew. Amen.

On the *red* bead closest to the crucifix, recite in your own words a prayer of thanksgiving:

I thank you, Jesus, for . . .

On the *white* bead closest to the crucifix, recite in your own words a prayer of petition:

I ask you, Jesus, for . . .

On the medal, pray an Our Father, to be said but once in this Rosary. On the circle of beads, you will cover these mysteries:

Joyful (blue): the annunciation, the visitation, and the nativity

Luminous (yellow): the baptism of Jesus, the wedding at Cana, the institution of the Eucharist

Sorrowful (red): the agony in the garden, the carrying of the cross, the crucifixion

Glorious (white): the resurrection, the descent of the Holy Spirit, the assumption

Starting with the joyful mysteries on the blue beads, announce the mystery, and read a scriptural meditation on the first separate bead. Next, pray three Hail Marys on the three closely grouped beads. Follow these with a simplified Glory Be on the chain:

Glory be to the Father, the Son, and the Holy Spirit. Amen.

After completing all twelve mysteries, conclude:

On the Fiat medal, recite the Fátima Prayer:

O my Jesus, forgive us our sins, save us from the fires of hell, and lead all souls to heaven, especially those in most need of thy (your) mercy.

On the *white* bead:

St. Joseph, guardian of the Holy Family, protect us.

On the *red* bead:

> St. Michael the archangel, from the powers of evil defend us.

On the *yellow* bead:

> All the angels and the saints, pray for us.

On the *blue* bead: the Prayer to Our Lady of the Fiat:

> O Mary, Our Lady of the Fiat, I place in the protection of your holy hands my going out, my coming in, my sleeping, my waking, the sight of my eyes, the touch of my hands, the speech from my lips, and the hearing of my ears, so that in everything I may be pleasing to you and your Beloved Son, Jesus. Amen.

End with the Sign of the Cross:

> In the name of the Father, and of the Son, and of the Holy Spirit. Amen.[18]

The Rosary in Various Situations

The Rosary at a Funeral Vigil

There is a strong tradition among Catholics of praying the Rosary during the wake at the funeral home the evening prior to the funeral Mass. The person leading the Rosary—often a priest, deacon, family member, or friend of the family—makes the Sign of the Cross and then recites the first part of the Apostles' Creed alone, up to the words "I believe in the Holy Spirit." At this point, the entire assembly joins in to complete the prayer.

The leader then begins each decade of the Rosary by announcing the mystery the decade honors. He or she recites each Our Father alone until the words "Give us this day" and each Hail Mary alone until the words "Holy Mary, Mother of God," and everyone joins in to complete the prayer. The leader closes each decade with "Glory be to the Father, and to the Son, and to the Holy Spirit," and everyone joins in with the concluding words of the prayer.

If the family of the deceased person wishes to include the Fátima prayer at the end of each Glory Be, the leader begins the prayer by saying: "O my Jesus, forgive us our sins." The assembly then joins in: "Save us from the fires of hell, and lead all souls to heaven, especially those in most need of thy (your) mercy. Amen."

Praying the Rosary as a Group

One of the great attractions of the Rosary is how easily it lends itself to being prayed by a group of almost any size. As described in the previous example, the standard way to do this is for one person (or a series of persons) to lead, saying the first half of the prayer, and the group joining in to complete it. Simple!

Praying the Rosary as a Family

Fr. Patrick Peyton, CSC, was the founder of the Family Rosary Crusade, a popular movement in the 1950s and early '60s. He coined the catchy slogan "The family that prays together stays together." Just so, countless families over the decades have found in the Rosary a source of spiritual nourishment and strength.

Praying the Rosary as a family has its special challenges, but it's always worth a try. Some families opt to pray the Rosary during Lent or on special occasions. Some pray the Rosary while driving on an extended family trip or vacation. Be creative!

The Children's Rosary

The Children's Rosary is a movement designed to help parishes establish Rosary prayer groups composed of and led by children between the ages of four and fourteen. The children to whom Mary appeared at Fátima and Bernadette, to whom Mary appeared at Lourdes, were all within this age range (see Appendix B). There is, however, flexibility at each end of the range, and children should never be turned away if they want to be part of a prayer group. Children with disabilities may be older in age, but they have a special place in the Children's Rosary and should be encouraged to be part of this prayer movement. Adults are always welcome and encouraged to come to the Children's Rosary.[19]

THE ROSARY AND THE MARIAN APPARITIONS OF LOURDES AND FÁTIMA

As of this writing, the Catholic Church has officially approved as authentic ten apparitions of the Blessed Virgin Mary. Official approval, however, does not mean Catholics must accept these events. The Church underscores that apparitions are private and do not add any additional material to the truths of the Catholic Church as expressed in *public* revelation, namely, Scripture and sacred Tradition. Individual believers may choose to accept these apparitions or not, according to their own discernment and needs.

Two of these approved apparitions, Our Lady of Lourdes (1858; approved 1870) and Our Lady of Fátima (1917; approved 1930), hold particular interest for some, probably many, devotees of the Rosary.

Our Lady of Lourdes

The most popular Marian apparition site in the world is in Lourdes, France, in the northern foothills of the French Pyrénées. On February 11, 1858, an illiterate young girl, Marie-Bernard Soubirous—known as "Bernadette"—was collecting firewood in the countryside with her sister and a friend. The day was cold, and the three girls were dressed in little more than rags as they scrounged for anything they could take home to burn for heat.

The other girls crossed a small stream to continue their search, but Bernadette, who was of delicate health, paused. As she considered her options, she noticed a "soft glow" in a hollowed-out area of a high rock cliff called Massabielle. Later she said that she had seen this soft glow in the same place twice before as she searched for firewood. This time, however, Bernadette saw a "small maiden" dressed in white and holding a golden rosary, standing in the glow. The young woman gestured to Bernadette to come closer, but Bernadette remained motionless with terror.

On their return, the other girls found their companion kneeling and staring up at the cave. They looked, trying to see what Bernadette was staring at, but they saw nothing unusual.

More apparitions followed, however, and the result for Bernadette was nothing but trouble and grief. The neighbors scolded her for making up ridiculous stories, and the village priest accused Bernadette of lying. On her next visit to Massabielle, Bernadette brought holy water from the parish church and tossed it at the apparition, thinking that if the young woman were a demon in disguise, the holy water would drive it away. Later Bernadette reported that when she did this, the "small maiden" smiled.

While Bernadette was sprinkling the apparition with holy water, a friend climbed up to the cliff and pushed a large rock over the edge. It landed with a thud near Bernadette, but she continued gazing at the vision undisturbed. In her regional

Bigourdan dialect, Bernadette referred to the beautiful young woman as *Aquero*, meaning "that one."

Before long, news of Bernadette's visions spread, and hundreds of people, then thousands, followed her to the grotto each day. On either February 25 or 26—reports are unclear—the woman instructed Bernadette to "drink of the spring," which in fact was nothing but muddy dirt just inside the cave. When Bernadette did so, water came up out of the ground. This stream eventually flowed into a nearby river, the Gave de Pau, producing twenty-five thousand gallons of fresh, clear water every twenty-four hours.

Within hours of the spring's appearance, a blind man washed his eyes in the water and was able to see again. A woman with a paralyzed hand plunged it into the water and regained full use of her hand.

At the insistence of the parish priest, Bernadette asked the young woman to reveal her name. Bernadette said that the woman laughed at her assertiveness and replied, after repeated requests, "*Que soy era l'Immaculada Concepciou*," "I am the Immaculate Conception."

The dogma of the Immaculate Conception—that Mary was free of original sin from the moment of her conception—had been defined by the Church only four years earlier, and it is highly unlikely that an uneducated country girl like Bernadette would have heard about it. The meaning of the title was explained to her over and over again in the days to come, but it was a long time—only after she had learned to read and write—before full comprehension sank in.

Bernadette was canonized a saint in 1933, and her feast day is April 14. The feast of Our Lady of Lourdes is February 11.

The connection between the Rosary and Lourdes began during the earliest days of Bernadette's visions, when she reported that the young woman appeared holding a golden rosary. Also, Bernadette was often seen silently praying the Rosary during the apparitions. The Rosary has become a common part of life in and around the shrine at Lourdes, and pilgrims are encouraged to pray it often. Each evening at 9:00 p.m., Lourdes becomes the site of a torchlight Marian procession, a custom practiced continuously since 1872. During the procession, participants pray the Rosary aloud in their native languages.

Our Lady of Fátima

Between May and October of 1917, while the world was embroiled in the horrors of World War I, three shepherd children in Portugal—Lucia Santos and her cousins, Francisco and Jacinta Marto—said that the Blessed Virgin Mary appeared to them six times.

The Fátima apparitions actually began in the spring of 1916 when, according to the children, a young man appeared to them and identified himself as the angel of peace. The angel taught them to pray and make sacrifices in a particular way; then he departed. During the next twelve months, the three children followed the instructions they were given. Then, on May 13, 1917, while watching over their flock of sheep near the Cova da Iria, they saw a beautiful lady dressed in white and surrounded by rays of brilliant light.

The woman told them not to be afraid and said she would return on the thirteenth day of each month, until October. At that time, the children said, she would reveal her identity and what she wanted them to do. The lady also told the children to pray the Rosary every day.

When members of the children's immediate and extended family learned about the children's experiences, they pressured them to deny the whole business and admit that they had made up their story. But the children remained firmly insistent that what they said was true. Most adults refused to believe that Mary would appear to mere children and tell them nothing more than to pray the Rosary. The lady promised the three little shepherds that she would give a sign that would convince those who persisted in their disbelief.

Meanwhile, the children continued going to the Cova da Iria on the thirteenth day of each month. They said that the lady announced that she wanted to have Russia dedicated to her Immaculate Heart. She also requested that people receive Holy Communion and go to Confession on the first Saturday of five successive months, in reparation for the sins of humanity.

During these visits, the children said, they also received apocalyptic visions and dire predictions about the future. The lady also gave them three "secrets," two of which were revealed to the public within the next decades, while the third remained undisclosed, raising speculation about its potentially terrifying content.

The final apparition occurred on October 13, 1917. On that day, the children said that the lady told them that she was "Our Lady of the Rosary" and that she wanted a shrine built on the site of her apparitions. As she disappeared from the children's sight, the crowd of some seventy thousand people that had gathered saw what has come to be called the "miracle of the sun." A tremendous downpour of rain had been going on, but it suddenly stopped, and the sun came out. People who were there reported that they saw the sun "dance" in the sky, then plunge toward the earth.

Subsequent study of this phenomenon leaves considerable doubt as to what actually happened, but regardless, many people were overcome by whatever did take place and fell to their knees in astonishment, crying out to God to save them. At this point, according to accounts, the sun returned to its place, and the rain-drenched pilgrims were suddenly dry and comfortable.

Meanwhile, back at the ranch, the three children said that at this time, they also saw visions of the Holy Family, Mary as the sorrowful mother with her son, and Mary as Our Lady of Mount Carmel.

The apparitions of Fátima were declared authentic by the bishop of Leiria on October 13, 1930. Interest in the Fátima story increased greatly, particularly during World War II and the subsequent rise of the Soviet Union. For decades, the famous "third secret" of Fátima was revealed only to popes; consequently, rumors and sensationalism ruled. Wild, unfounded stories circulated about popes reading the "third secret" and fainting dead away. Other equally fantastic stories said that the pope always kept the "third secret" locked in his private quarters or concealed on his own person at all times.

The truth is that the "third secret" was passed along from one pope to another down to the present time, and each decided whether to reveal the secret or not. In the year 2000, Pope St. John Paul II finally made public the contents of the "third secret." Commenting on it, Lucia, by this time a ninety-three-year-old nun, said that the secret concerns above all the struggle of atheistic Communism against the Church and against Christians and describes the great persecutions and sufferings of the faithful in the twentieth century.

The traditional representation of Our Lady of Fátima shows her in a simple gown and mantle of white bordered with blue, her hands folded in prayer and holding a white rosary. She is always depicted wearing a jeweled crown. The feast of Our Lady of Fátima is May 13.

Again, Catholics are free to attend to or disregard the apparitions at Lourdes and Fátima. At the very least, both may be taken as encouragement to pray the Rosary. Particularly with regard to Fátima, however, it may be prudent to take apocalyptic "prophecies" and "promises" with a grain of salt. It remains essential to repeat that these are private revelation that may or may not contribute to a healthy faith. Charity requires that we respect the decisions of others to incorporate—or not—the events at Lourdes and Fátima into their own spirituality.

Finally, it is important to note that in May 2017, Pope Francis canonized two of the three Portuguese shepherd children—Jacinta Marto and her brother, Francisco—on the centennial of the Fátima apparitions.

Appendix C

A Rosary Testimony

To describe all of the ways people have found to use the Rosary would take another book. But the following story by Lynn Morales should give you at least a few ideas of how the Rosary could be adapted to your life. A convert to Catholicism, Lynn started praying the Rosary only recently. For Lynn—like the rest of us—the hardest part was getting started. But once she made the effort, she found creative ways both to pray the Rosary and to fit it into her busy days. Even more, she found it to be a source of inspiration and closeness to God. What more could any of us want?

* * *

I am a stay-at-home mom, and I've prayed the Rosary for about a year now. It has been such a blessing. I am a convert to the Catholic faith, and I used to look at the Rosary as something "too Catholic," too hard to do, and worst of all—boring!

The blessing is that while the Rosary may seem like a rote prayer, I discovered that the more I do it, the more the Holy Spirit illuminates my faith and leads me to pray and intercede for myself, my family, and others. It has strengthened my relationship with our Lord. Every day I look forward to where the Rosary will lead me.

I try to say the Rosary after I drop my kids off at school, but the beauty of the Rosary is its flexibility. Many times I will start the Rosary in the morning and not finish it until I am in bed. Sometimes I can just say one decade at different times of the day because I am rushing around. This calms me and reminds me to make everything a prayer.

After I drop off my children at school, I have a precious half hour for the commute home. I used to dread the ride home because I sit in traffic, but now it's my special time with the Lord and Mary. I start the Rosary right after my last child shuts the door. I always wonder if someone who sees me might think that I have rascals for children, since I always make the Sign of the Cross as I pull out of the school parking lot!

I dedicate the first mystery to my husband, our marriage, and my vocation as a wife. I ask the Lord to bless him as a husband and father and help me to love and serve him. After twelve years of marriage, you might think that I would have this down, but the Rosary nudges me to love my spouse in a deeper way.

For the second mystery, I pray for my five children—especially for holiness or for a particular struggle that they are going through. If I know that they have something important happening in their lives, like a test or report due for school, I tell them that I will pray the Rosary for them. I try to remind the kids that I pray to Mary to intercede for them, so that they know that I take the time to think and pray for them. Many times this leads me to new insights with my children. I hope that, in the chaos of daily life, it comforts them to know that their mom lifts them up in prayer to our Blessed Mother.

The third mystery I dedicate to my extended family and friends. I ask the Lord, "Whom should I pray for?" I am amazed at the people who come into my thoughts as I pray. Many times I will be inspired to take action when these intentions come up.

I call the fourth mystery my "dandelion patch." Just as a lawn may have several dandelions that break up a nice landscape, I pray in the fourth mystery that the Lord will help me pull up any "dandelions" like petty grudges, judgments, or anger. I firmly believe that the Lord wants us to be "sweet soil" and that holding on to little or big grudges takes up precious room where his Holy Spirit wants to put down roots and grow in us. If you don't pull out the "dandelions," even if they look harmless, they will take up room and spread.

For instance, I will pray for someone who has made negative comments about my children and ask the Lord to forgive my bitter feelings. Unforgiveness, anger, and bitterness take root easily—so I try to yank out these "dandelions" every day. Sometimes it seems as if the same old weeds keep coming up, but with the Rosary, it gets easier to spot them and remove them.

For the fifth mystery, I pray for my parish priests and for vocations. I also try to pray for our country and for wisdom for our president and his cabinet.

I made a commitment that if I was praying the Rosary while I was driving and I mumbled, grumbled, or glared nastily toward other drivers, I would start the decade over. Driving in the Washington, DC, area, I have had many opportunities to start over!

There are so many different ways to pray the Rosary. On Saturdays I do what I call a "potpourri Rosary," which means that I think about the fruit of a certain mystery and see where the Holy Spirit leads me to pray. For instance, the first joyful mystery is the annunciation, and a fruit of that mystery is humility. I try to pray for humility for myself or for some other person who comes to mind. I love the idea that each mystery has a "fruit." When I think of fruit, I think of how nourishing it is for your body. I feel like I get nourished with fresh fruit from the Rosary every day.

The fruits of the mysteries of the Rosary are not what the world idolizes, such as intelligence, wealth, or power. For example, the fruits of the sorrowful mysteries are sorrow for sin, purity, courage, patience, and—my favorite mystery and fruit—perseverance. These fruits remind me of what is important to our Lord and his kingdom.

Another way I have started to pray the Rosary is based on the idea that there are five "p's" in the lives of mothers—prayer, person, partner, parent, and provider—as outlined in Holly Pierlot's book *A Mother's Rule of Life*.[20] After I read this book, I thought I would take these five "p's" to the Rosary. So for the first mystery (prayer), I pray that I grow closer to our Lord in prayer, or I pray for anyone else I know who I think needs to draw closer to him. Sometimes I ask, "Is my prayer life okay with you, Lord? Am I doing too much, too little? Should I read something new?"

For the second mystery (person), I pray that I take care of my body so I can be available for the Lord, or I pray for someone else's spiritual, mental, or physical health. Sometimes my prayer is as simple as "Lord, I need a good night's sleep. Please help me get to bed early."

For the third mystery (partner), I pray for my spouse and that I can love and see him as our Lord does.

For the fourth mystery (parent), I pray for my children and for my friends' children. Many times I will pray for my children's future spouses, especially that they will be holy and kind. Many times I will thank the Lord just for giving me perseverance with my children, since I don't always feel successful as a parent.

For the fifth mystery (provider), I pray that I will fulfill my vocation as a wife and mother. With this last decade, I pray that I don't let chores around the house or other things overshadow my presence to my family. I feel so energized when I get things done that I sometimes neglect my family in the process. The love-to-get-things-done side of me sometimes would rather send out another e-mail, finish laundry, or clean the bathroom rather than play games or read books with my children.

Sometimes, like a physical workout, beginning the Rosary is the hardest part for me, but I'm always fortified when I do it. Often, I feel like I don't say the Rosary "right" because of distraction or fatigue, but I never regret praying the Rosary, even if I have to muddle through. What mother doesn't want her child to come to her? Mother Mary is always available. Discover the Rosary, and see where Mary will lead you—right to Jesus, her son.

NOTES

1. Catholic News Service, April 26, 2006.

2. Adapted from the Rosary Foundation, erosary.com/rosary/benefits/mental.htm.

3. H. Thurston and A. Shipman, "The Rosary," in the *Catholic Encyclopedia* (New York: Robert Appleton, 1912), newadvent.org.

4. Thurston and Shipman.

5. Shawn Madigan, CSJ, "Rosary," in Michael Downey, ed., *The New Dictionary of Catholic Spirituality* (Collegeville, MN: Liturgical, 1993), 150.

6. "The Rosary Since Vatican II," *The Marian Library Newsletter,* Spring 1995.

7. Fr. John L. McKenzie, *Dictionary of the Bible* (Milwaukee: Bruce, 1965), 194.

8. Blaise Pascal, *Pensées,* § IV, 273 (New York: Penguin, 1995), 54.

9. John W. Miller, *Calling God "Father": Essays on the Bible, Fatherhood & Culture* (New York: Paulist, 1999), 5.

10. Fr. Raymond Brown, SS, *New Testament Essays* (New York: Paulist, 1965), 279.

11. Thurston, "Hail Mary," *Catholic Encyclopedia,* vol. 7.

12. *Merriam-Webster's Collegiate Dictionary,* eleventh ed. (Springfield, MA: Merriam-Webster, 2011), 822.

13. Fr. Robert P. Maloney, CM, "The Historical Mary," *America,* December 19–26, 2005.

14. Sherman Alexie, "Drum as Love, Fear, Prayer," in *The Summer of Black Widows* (New York: Hanging Loose, 1996). Used with permission.

15. Vatican II, Dogmatic Constitution on the Church, 59, in Austin Flannery, ed., *Vatican Council II, Volume 1: The Conciliar and Post Conciliar Documents,* rev. ed. (Northport, NY: Costello, 1996), 418.

16. L. J. Cardinal Suenens, *The Hidden Hand of God: Life of Veronica O'Brien and Our Common Apostolate* (Veritas, 1994). Also found at thefiatrosary.com/history/.

17. The Fiat Rosary: A Rosary for Our Times, thefiatrosary.com/history/.

18. The instructions are adapted with permission from thefiatrosary.com/. Consult this website for more information on the Fiat Rosary.

19. Adapted with permission from childrensrosary.com/ and childrensrosary.blogspot.com/. Extensive information about the Children's Rosary is available on these two sites.

20. Holly Pierlot, *A Mother's Rule of Life* (Manchester, NH: Sophia, 2004).

the WORD among us®
The *Spirit* of Catholic Living

This book was published by The Word Among Us. Since 1981, The Word Among Us has been answering the call of the Second Vatican Council to help Catholic laypeople encounter Christ in the Scriptures.

The name of our company comes from the prologue to the Gospel of John and reflects the vision and purpose of all of our publications: to be an instrument of the Spirit, whose desire is to manifest Jesus' presence in and to the children of God. In this way, we hope to contribute to the Church's ongoing mission of proclaiming the gospel to the world so that all people would know the love and mercy of our Lord and grow ever more deeply in love with him.

Our monthly devotional magazine, *The Word Among Us*, features meditations on the daily and Sunday Mass readings, and currently reaches more than one million Catholics in North America and another half million Catholics in one hundred countries around the world. Our book division, The Word Among Us Press, publishes numerous books, Bible studies, and pamphlets that help Catholics grow in their faith.

To learn more about who we are and what we publish, log on to our website at www.wau.org. There you will find a variety of Catholic resources that will help you grow in your faith.

Embrace His Word, Listen to God . . .

www.wau.org